MAGNOLIA
A VIEW OF HEAVEN

THOMAS FARGNOLI

Copyright © 2024 Thomas Fargnoli

All rights reserved.

No part of this publication in print or in electronic format may be reproduced, stored in a retrieval system, or transmitted in any form or by any means, electronic, mechanical, photocopying, recording, or otherwise without the prior written permission of the publisher.

This is a work of fiction. Names, characters, organizations, places, events and incidents are either the products of the author's imagination or are used fictitiously. Any resemblance to actual persons, living or dead, or actual events is purely coincidental.

Editing, design, and distribution by Bublish
Published by Thomas Fargnoli Books

ISBN: 978-1-647048-05-1 (paperback)
ISBN: 978-1-647048-06-8 (eBook)

CONTENTS

Note to the Reader | v

Dedication | vii

CHAPTER 1   *A First Glimpse* | 1
CHAPTER 2   *Am I in Heaven?* | 6
CHAPTER 3   *The Peace of Magnolia* | 18
CHAPTER 4   *Where Am I?* | 29
CHAPTER 5   *Welcome to the Spiritual Realm* | 39
CHAPTER 6   *Fruits of the Spirit* | 52
CHAPTER 7   *God Assignments* | 61
CHAPTER 8   *There Is Only Now* | 73
CHAPTER 9   *I Feel You* | 83
CHAPTER 10   *A Nobody from New Jersey* | 95
CHAPTER 11   *In the Flow* | 105
CHAPTER 12   *Love Never Dies* | 115

Afterword | 131

NOTE TO THE READER

Magnolia—A View of Heaven is a work of fiction. While it features a real town (Magnolia, New Jersey) and some of its past and present locations and establishments, it reflects the author's views derived from his childhood while growing up in Magnolia. With respect to heaven and what it might be like, it also reflects the author's views. All aspects are strictly fictional, and any names used do not reflect actual people. Opinions expressed are entirely those of the author.

Having said all that, I believe my view of heaven is a reasonable one. I base that on various accounts, writings, and what is in my heart. Of course, no one can say whether I am right or wrong, but I present my views with the intent of providing the reader with hope—hope based on peace, love, and joy.

DEDICATION

This book is dedicated to all your loved ones who have moved into the spiritual realm. Eternal rest grant unto them, O Lord, and let perpetual light shine upon them. May their souls, through the mercy of God, rest in peace.

CHAPTER 1

A First Glimpse

> Love is perhaps the only glimpse
> we are permitted of eternity.
> —Helen Hayes

THE WARMTH OF sunlight filtering through the canopy of a giant oak tree collapses over my shoulders like an embrace. I sit on a wooden bench, elbows leaning on the attached picnic table, and listen to the sound of acorns falling around me—some even hitting the table. Looking up, I shield my eyes from the sparkling sunlight that falls in fingerlike shafts between branches oscillating in the breeze.

Peace permeates my being. Doves coo softly alongside a myriad of songbirds. Their joyful symphony makes me think that even the birds are enjoying this peace.

Breathing deeply, I smell the fragrance of sweet magnolia blossoms and—

Wait, what is that? Ah yes. *Roses.*

An orchestra of sweet floral scents lifts my spirit. I can't help but smile as I breathe in the aroma, and suddenly it dawns on me that I am taking deep breaths without pain and without coughing. I haven't done that in such a long time. No, I don't want to analyze these moments; I just want to enjoy the peace and tranquility I am immersed in. I have never felt so peaceful and so free of anxiety. To my left is a large flowering dogwood tree, lit up by the same gentle caress of the sunlight.

Suddenly, I realize there is something very familiar about this place. For a moment, a spike of unrest zips through my body. A memory flashes before my mind's eye: a Tarzan rope my father hung for me on the oak tree's strongest arm. I recall being here at night, the sulfur-scented glimmer of a sparkler in my hand and fireworks bursting like popcorn in the sky.

This is the yard I grew up in. I am in Magnolia.

I get up and walk across the emerald-green lawn toward the oak tree, and as I do, I notice that to my right is an amazing garden with many ripe tomatoes, red and green bell peppers, and other produce. The garden is enclosed by a small wire fence. I decide to go view the garden rather than the oak tree for now and, upon getting closer, detect a certain fragrance emanating from the area that must be the tomatoes.

A basket rests inside the small fence. Memories of picking the ripe tomatoes and peppers and placing them in the basket start to trickle into my mind. Such great memories. It felt great to have certain responsibilities around the house, and picking tomatoes and peppers was one of them. I had two other chores: burning the trash and burning leaves—two tasks unheard of in today's world, especially for a twelve-year-old boy.

More memories start to pour into my mind as I walk around to the back of the garden, outside the small fence. Two raspberry bushes and a blackberry bush with ripe berries, almost yearning to be picked and eaten, bring a smile to my face. Kneeling, I pick a few of the raspberries. They are so soft in my hand—their centers staying with the stem, leaving me with a hollow fruit. As I put one in my mouth, the taste explodes across my tongue. Yes, I've eaten these raspberries before. There is a freshness to them, but their tart undertone makes their sweetness subtler than, say, a cherry.

My eyes wander over the raspberry and blackberry bushes and, feeling the strange, delightful nostalgia they evoke, I know I'd be perfectly happy to sit around all day, eating each and every berry off these branches. But it's been years—decades—since I've spent any time here in this yard, and I've missed it.

I'm eager to go see the rest before I wake up from this dream.

Surely I am dreaming, right?

Walking around to the backside of the garden, I spot a small, unofficial orchard of plum trees and a large peach tree. My hand reaches autonomously toward the plum tree, which was my favorite growing up, and brushes against the silver-brown bark of it.

Surely, this is a dream, I think again. *A dream I'm in no hurry to wake up from.*

I move my tongue across my teeth and gums, the taste of raspberries so very real, and wonder if I've ever had a dream as convincing as this one—as lucid. I could live here for days, weeks. Growing up in this backyard was one of the happiest eras of my life.

As I pick a purple plum, I realize this was always my favorite fruit in the yard. I bite into the plump meat of the fruit and look at the adjacent peach tree bordering my yard and the Baitengers'.

I think about all the times I sat on their open front porch in a rocking chair, talking to old man Baitenger while enjoying a summer day.

Putting that thought aside, I pick a peach and eat it—fuzzy skin and all—and toss the pit on the ground.

Another flowering dogwood tree is to my right, this one, a beautiful shade of pink. Between me and the pink dogwood, rows of many varieties of roses have bloomed. I pause before a rosebush that strikes me as the most familiar; it releases an exceptional and unique fragrance, unlike any rosebush I have ever smelled. The roses are smaller and flatter than most, and there are many Japanese beetles on them.

"I remember you guys," I say, putting one of the beetles on my finger. I slowly curl my hand around it, cupping it, and after a minute or so, I reopen my hand and smile as I see a few drops of brown liquid. I remember my dad telling me, "If you hold a Japanese beetle in your hand, it will spit on you."

I place the beetle back on the rosebush and tell him, "I guess I'm not the only one who enjoys the smell of these roses."

Leaning closer to one of the bushes, I take in its amazing aroma, letting it permeate my whole being. *Everything is just so perfect here.*

The aroma stays with me as I gaze back to the oak tree, and another memory trickles in. *There it is!* The Tarzan rope. I remember my dad and Uncle Bill sitting at the picnic table, saying, "Okay, Louie, there is a lion in front of the house. He sees you and is running toward you. How fast can you climb up that rope?"

They'd laugh as they drank their beers, watching me scurry all the way up that rope to the high branch to avoid the lion and then come back down. I couldn't help but laugh at the memory, but as my laughter subsided, I looked at the rope and thought, *What the hell?*

Those berries and plums tasted real, and the smell of the roses still lingered in my nostrils. *I'm going for it!* It's been so long since I've run, let alone sprinted, and seeing as this surely is a dream, that means I am capable of anything, right?

I run like the wind toward the rope, grabbing it and holding it tight as my momentum takes me way up in the air. When I swing back down, there's a split second of zero gravity right before I'm pulled back toward the earth again. *I've forgotten this. I've forgotten what this felt like.* And best of all, I do this with the alacrity of youth. I don't have any pain in my body or joints, any stiffness in my muscles.

When I've had my fill, leaping off the rope after several ups and downs, I step back onto the springy, lime-green lawn and survey the area once more—the oak tree with that familiar picnic table stationed beneath its tangled canopy and the garden with its ripe fruit and bright colors. *I'd like to stay here forever.*

In fact, I think I'd like another plum.

As I start to walk back toward the plum tree, my steps become labored, and the roses' fragrance starts to go sour. It becomes harder for me to breathe, and all of a sudden, my chest feels painful and tight—another familiar feeling, but this time far less nostalgic.

I begin coughing, trying to clear the tightness in my chest. The peace of this sacred place is drained away with each cough. My energy level is no longer that of a twelve-year-old but of a ninety-two-year-old, and from someplace close to me, I hear a voice saying, "Dad? Are you okay?"

CHAPTER 2

Am I in Heaven?

> Therefore, we are not discouraged; rather,
> although our outer self is wasting away, our
> inner self is being renewed day by day.
> —2 Corinthians 4:16

IN A BLINK, my childhood backyard disappears and is replaced by a bleary-eyed view of my own gray-haired arms. I note the dark purple and black bruises from recent IVs. Are these the same arms that just held the Tarzan rope, strong enough to support me effortlessly as I swung so high in the air? The same arms that allowed me to get away from the lion? Now, they are frail and listless. My eyes trace the tube from my forearm to the IV bag of God knows what.

Every breath I take is punctuated by a wheeze.

Again, I hear, "Dad? Are you okay?"

"Mikey?" As my eyes come into focus, I see my son looking down at me.

"Looks like you were struggling to breathe there for a while, Pop."

"Yeah, I . . ." As I begin to speak, I am cut off by a series of uncontrollable coughs and struggle to catch my breath.

"It's okay, Dad. Just relax. Don't try to talk."

After a while, I regain my composure. "Damn cough. It hurts my chest when I cough like that, but I can't control it." It's scary, how hard it is to get a single sentence out without throwing myself into another coughing fit. "How are you, Mike? And the family?"

"Everybody's good, Pop. They all said to say hi and that they are praying for you."

Still struggling to breathe without coughing, I say, "That's nice. Could you raise the bed up a bit for me, Mike? You would not believe where I just was. Well, in my dream, I suppose."

After raising the bed up, Mike smiles and asks, "Where did you go?"

Between breaths, I try and explain the best I can. "I believe I was in Magnolia—back in the house I grew up in. Well, not actually in the house; I was in the yard. The yard was just as it was when I was . . . oh, I don't know, ten or twelve. The oak tree was there, and my Tarz—" Again, coughing interrupts my speech. Mike waits patiently for me to regain my composure, but I can see the fear and sadness in his eyes. "My Tarzan rope," I go on, wheezing. "The one my dad put up for me was there, and I actually swung on it again."

My laughter turns into coughing.

Mike raises his brows. "You swung on the Tarzan rope?"

"I did. And I climbed it. It was so *real*, Mike. I also ate raspberries and a plum," I went on, wheezing again. "This damn cough . . . . Yes. It was all so real, Mike. I didn't cough, and I had no pain, and I felt so full of energy." Licking my lips, I continue, "I really tasted the fruit, and I smelled the roses."

"Sounds like you had an amazing dream, Pop," Mike said, grinning.

"It was so real," I say again. "I've never had a dream like that before."

"Maybe it was from all the drugs they're giving you through that IV."

"Well, if that's the case, I hope they keep giving me more. I felt so full of energy. Not like now."

Just talking about my dream is exhausting, and already I have to fight to keep my eyes open. I try to stay awake for my son, but it's so difficult, and I know the coughs will start again if I try to talk too much. "I'm so sorry, Mike. I . . ." I feel myself drifting away as I give in to my exhaustion, eyelids too heavy to keep open.

"You sleep, Pop. I'm going to grab something to eat in the cafeteria, and then I'll come back up. Want me to lower the bed?"

Before I can respond, a man walks into my room carrying a small book. He introduces himself to me and my son. "Hi, I am Chaplain Frank. I visit the patients here and see how they're doing—check if they need anything and also let them know we care about them. I can say a prayer for you if you'd like."

As the chaplain opens his little prayer book, Mike says, "Yeah, that would be nice, but I have to get something to eat. I'll be back in a half hour, Pop. Nice meeting you, Chaplain." Mike smiles at me as he leaves.

"You'll have to excuse my coughing, Chaplain, but it's uncontrollable. I appreciate you stopping by and, well, if you really want to say a prayer, why not?"

The chaplain looks at me and says, "Sure, but first, tell me something about yourself." He looks at his roster of patients, then addresses me. "Louis Bowella, is it?"

"That's me. Not much to tell. I am ninety-two and on my third bout of pneumonia. That was my son Mike who just left."

"Nice-looking man. He seemed very concerned about you."

"Yeah, he's a great guy, and he has a great family, with two teenage girls—" Another coughing fit interrupts us. "Sorry about that."

"No need to apologize, Lou. Is it okay if I call you Lou?"

"Sure, that's what most people call me." After a pause, I look at the chaplain in a serious way, before he picks out one of his prayers. "Perhaps you can say a prayer for my son, Chaplain."

"Call me Frank, Lou. I can certainly do that. Is there anything in particular?"

Something about Frank made me feel super relaxed and, for whatever reason, prompted me to tell him about our family. "The short story, Frank, is that my wife is gone almost thirty years now, and it has been a very difficult time for us and especially for Mike."

"I take it you were very close."

"Yes, but the difficulty started before she passed. Our other son, Timmy, drowned while camping with his friends. He was only thirteen." Tears flow as they always do when I talk about Timmy. "You see, Frank, it was my fault. I should never have let him go. He was too young for that trip. Jill, my wife, didn't want him to go. We argued about it, but in the end, it was me that pushed for him to go."

Frank closed his prayer book and placed his hand on my arm, amid the dark purple marks from the needles. "It wasn't your fault Timmy drowned, Lou. This world is full of choices we make every day. I am sure Timmy is in a good place, and I am also sure he doesn't fault you for the accident."

"I wish I could believe that, Frank. I wish my wife and I could have believed that so many years ago. The truth is that our marriage suffered after the accident. I don't think Jill ever forgave me for letting him go on that trip and all of it—well, it affected Mike. That's why he left as soon as he saw your prayer book. He wants nothing to do with God or prayer. He—" More coughing as I hold my chest. "He is convinced that no God could let that happen."

"And you, Lou, how is your faith?"

"My faith? I am bitter, I am mad at God for not just the accident but all the results."

"The results?"

"We were the perfect family, Frank. Jill was always so joyful. We went to church; we prayed together." Tears start flowing as I picture our once-perfect life. "So, slowly but surely, that joy we once had started to dissipate. We stopped going to church and praying. Jill, who was always the source of our joy, became—well, she became brokenhearted. My son believes it was her broken heart that took her life."

Frank, still holding my arm, looked at me intensely. "That is truly a sad story, Lou. An unexpected death, especially of a child, can certainly demolish your faith. You and your son have lived with this bitterness far too long."

"I wish I could wash it away, Frank, more for Mike's benefit than for mine. I don't want him to have this bitterness. Jill used to have such a lightness about her—such a joyfulness. It was contagious. Why would God take that away? I am old and close to the end, but I want that joy back for my son. Is that prayer in your little book?"

"Have you talked to God about this?"

"I used to, but whatever we did after Timmy and now after Jill—no matter what we try and do, we always fall short of happiness. I guess I gave up on it, and, as far as Mike goes, well, God is just not real to him."

"There is still time, Lou."

After another coughing spell and holding my chest, I look up at Frank. "Does that sound like there is time left?"

"Prayer is just talking to God, Lou. But you can talk to God by talking to your son. Tell him what's in your heart. Wouldn't you feel better knowing Mike is happier? Whether you live for ten more years or ten more minutes, wouldn't that give you joy?"

Looking at Frank and visualizing Mike happy and full of joy, I nod in agreement.

"You want a prayer? I have one, but it's not in my little book. I pray that you have the chance to talk to Mike and tell him how you feel. God doesn't cause these accidents to happen. In this world, people will continue to have accidents, but God loves you nonetheless, and he loves Mike, and he loves Timmy. You see, Lou, love never dies. Timmy and Jill are at peace. Believe me. Talk to Mike. Let him know how much you love him, and share your thoughts about Timmy with him while you are still here with him. That's my prayer, my friend. God is real, and there is still time to open Mike's heart to that reality. That joy is closer than you think."

"Closer than I think? I don't want to leave Mike and his family. I worry about them. I truly want them to be happy. I hope my bitterness didn't hurt them. You say talk to my son. What words can I use, Frank? I appreciate your concern, and I do feel your sincerity, but this hurt has been around for so long."

"I understand, Lou. Just talk to him. God will help you with the words."

Fatigue grows as I listen to Frank, but when I try to talk, I only manage to say a bunch of gibberish.

"Rest, my friend. Breathe deeply under the warm rays of sun that stream through the large oak tree." Frank smiles and leaves my room.

"Yes . . . back in Magnolia." Then I lose the battle of consciousness and fall into a deep sleep.

The pain in my chest subsides, and I can breathe deeply without coughing. I can feel my energy levels rising. And suddenly, I feel the warmth of the picnic table under my forearms and the sunlight on my shoulders—that sense of peace I felt before returning slowly but surely.

I look again at my arms; the purple and black bruises from the hospital are gone, my skin is smoother, and my gray arm hair is more of a light brown. I look over at the dogwood tree and then at the oak tree, confirming that I am where I was before: back in Magnolia, in the backyard of the house I grew up in.

I sit there for a few minutes, enjoying the lack of pain and deep breathing without coughing, before I look toward my house: a large, three-story home amid the magnolia, cherry, dogwood, and maple trees. The back door faces the right side of the house and has steps leading down to a cement path that runs to the front. At the bottom of the steps is a rock garden decorated with various flowers and shimmering rocks. I remember my mom telling me that many of them had mica in them, which made them glimmer.

From the garden to the front of the house are peonies in clusters of red, white, and pink petals.

Walking effortlessly down the path, again imbued with the energy of my younger self, I spot four large evergreens along the edge of our property. I remember hiding in those trees when we played jailbreak. Between the evergreen trees and my house stands a huge cherry tree. My mom used to get angry at the birds that ate those cherries and then painted the white cement path with their . . . well, with the digested cherries.

I glance over my shoulder and spot a black Schwinn bike. That was *my* bike! I lived on that bike, riding from one end of Magnolia to the other. Of course, Magnolia is just one square mile, but growing up, it felt massive. Regardless of its size, Magnolia was the perfect town for a boy to grow up in. The school, the playgrounds, the woods, the candy stores and bakery, the events—yes, one square mile of friendliness.

Memories start to flood my mind the second I touch the bike. My hands grip the handlebars, and it's as though no time has passed at all—as though just yesterday, I was riding this bike before dawn to deliver papers across Magnolia and heading to Bob's for penny candy or Nick and John's corner delicatessen in the afternoons.

I reflect back on my last visit to Magnolia. My last real visit—when I swung from my Tarzan rope, feasted on fresh fruit—and I appreciate the pace of this place more than I ever have before. *If I was able to swing on my Tarzan rope, why wouldn't I be able to go for a ride on my bike?*

Without thinking twice, I swing a leg over the bike and pedal down the side path to the street—my street—Lincoln Avenue. The air rushes through my hair and smells like honeysuckle and roses and summer break, and I can't stop smiling. *Now, which way do I go? Left toward Magnolia Public School or right and across the train tracks, hanging a left toward Nick and John's? Nick and John's it is! I wonder if those nickel candy bars are still on display? Why wouldn't they be, when everything else is exactly the way it once was?*

As I ride across the tracks on my bike, feeling the vibrations ripple through my body—without any pain or discomfort in my joints—I recall playing on the parked boxcars, looking for rocks to give to Nancy, who lived just around the corner from me. Just thinking about her brings a smile to my face; I always had a crush on her.

I turn left on Atlantic Avenue toward Nick and John's and the center of town—the ease of movement is like an ointment to my soul—and think to myself, *Clark bar, here I come!* Just the thought of milk chocolate and a crunchy peanut butter center makes my mouth water. I had many other favorites, including Butterfinger, Almond Joy, KitKat, and so many more. In fact, I loved sweets so much when I was younger that it's a wonder I have any teeth left at all.

I park my bike in front of Nick and John's and go in. Just as I savored the fragrance of the white roses at home, I savor the smell of cold cuts and fresh rolls, breathing in the nostalgic scent deeply, without pain. Reaching into my pocket for change, I find a quarter, a dime, and two pennies. *Let's see . . . I can get a hoagie for thirty-five cents or a bunch of candy.* What the hell. I go with candy. I don't think I have to worry about cavities at ninety-two, and even if I did, I don't think you can get a cavity in a dream.

I look over the rows of candy bars at the counter and spend the dime on two—a Clark bar and a Chunky, which is a big chunk of chocolate with peanuts and raisins wrapped in shiny foil. I hand the money over to Don, one of the sons of either Nick or John. He smiles at me, as if he knows I am dreaming and he is a part of it. As I prepare to leave, I notice the gumball machine at the front door.

How had I forgotten about the gumball machine?

I walk up, studying gumballs of all colors inside its glass bubble. Amid the solid-colored ones, there are a few that are multicolored, which are considered prizes. If you get one of those, you can exchange it for a five-cent candy bar or a pack of baseball cards that come with a powdered rectangle of pink bubble gum. I recall chewing that gum as I looked through the cards, hoping for a Phillies player. Again, I think to myself, *Oh, what the hell? Let's go for it.*

I slide a penny into the machine's coin slot and turn the knob, yielding me a yellow gumball, which I throw into my mouth immediately, biting through the hard sugar shell and right into the bubble gum. I would say the taste brings me back, but I am already back.

Giggling aloud, I insert my last penny and turn the knob. Opening the cover after hearing the gumball hit, I see a multi-colored one. *Yes!* Don gives me a smirk, knowing I got the rainbow gumball. I hand it to him, exchanging it for a Mallo Cup, one of my favorites of all time. A coconut-laced milk chocolate cup that contains a whipped marshmallow center. It's more like whipped cream than marshmallow, though, and inside there is a cardboard coin representing "Mallo Cup points." I never collected them but always gazed at them as I enjoyed the milk chocolate and whipped marshmallow.

Just before walking out, I notice the sodas in the refrigerator box. Opening the top, I see just about every type you can imagine. In addition to Pepsi and Coke, there are lime, orange, chocolate, root beer, and my favorite—cream soda. For fifteen cents, I can't resist. Walking out, I put the Chunky and Clark bar in my pocket, mount my trusty Schwinn, and eat my Mallo Cup while I ride, pausing only briefly to wash it down with cream soda.

I feel like a king.

I finish my soda and toss the bottle in a trash bin, thinking to myself, *I have everything I need. Well, except for one more thing . . .*

My eyes glide automatically across the street to the Magnolia Bakery. Oh, the smells from that bakery. *I wonder if they still have those fifteen-cent brownies?* Again, I think about how this is a dream, and, in reality, I'm struggling to breathe in a hospital bed at the age of ninety-two. I'd be a fool not to make another stop and enjoy myself.

I shove off from the curb, crossing Evesham Road and riding up the bakery driveway, dismounting my bike like a cowboy would dismount his trusty horse. Throwing the kickstand down, I walk into the bakery, knowing exactly where the brownies are. I breathe in all the fresh-baked cakes and pies, believing very much that this has to be one of the most heavenly dreams I've ever had, and approach a small countertop with a woman behind it. She's wearing a blue checkerboard smock over a white blouse and smiling at me as though she knows me.

"Are you still selling those fifteen-cent brownies?" I ask. I'm surprised to hear the pitch of my voice. It's young, just like my body.

"Still?" the lady working there asked, cocking a brow. "We never stopped."

"I'll have a brownie, then," I say.

"That will be fifteen cents, hon."

Hon? I just smile and offer her a dime and nickel, and she hands me a fresh-cut brownie wrapped in parchment paper. I accept it happily and walk back outside, the shop's door closing with the ring of a bell. The midsummer sunlight is harsh in the very best way—the way that makes me think of the freedom of summer break, the smell of swimming in the lake, and the chime of the ice cream truck.

I hop on my bike and take my first bite of the fresh-baked brownie, practically moaning over the deliciousness of it. Moist, fudgy, dense, and gooey—it's almost the texture of fudge but not quite as compact.

I pause, listening to the sounds of summer birds, distant music, and the soft strum of the breeze filtering through the trees. Somebody nearby is barbecuing, the savory scent of grilled meat and vegetables tied into the wind, alongside my favorite honeysuckle-and-rose underlay.

As I chew my brownie, absorbing this beautiful setting, a profound thought strikes me: *Am I in heaven?* Then, an even more profound thought ensues: *I hope so. I never want to leave this place.*

Oh, the joy of riding my bike with no hands as I take out my Clark bar, peel its wrapping off like a banana, and take a bite. The joy flows through me and bubbles over as I head down Evesham Road toward Bob's.

Talk about candy. That's the place to go. He has a whole section of penny candy from Red Hots to Mary Janes, from string licorice to Pixy Stix, from Nik-L-Nips (wax bottles filled with flavored syrup) to Twizzlers, licorice laces, and so much more.

On the way, I ride by a Sinclair gas station and spontaneously decide to ride over the bell-signal hose. This always pisses off the attendant, for he has to stop working on an engine and come out to pump gas.

But who cares? This is probably heaven. My heaven.

I fly over the signal, laughing as I hear the ding-ding, ding-ding of the bell chiming behind me. I don't look back and continue toward Bob's a little faster, laughing as I ride. Looking down as I pedal, I appreciate how strong my legs are again and how much energy I have. *Boy, did I take this for granted when I was young.* So engrossed in my legs, I fail to notice a parked pickup truck and plow right into it.

The truck is just short enough for my bike to snag while my body flies over the handlebars, flipping me into the bed of the pickup.

I lie there a moment, gasping for breath. *I can't breathe. I can't breathe.*

I must've knocked the air out of my lungs. But the more I try, the harder it gets, and the edges of my vision begin to blur.

Just as I think, *I'm going to pass out*, I do, and everything fades to black.

CHAPTER 3

The Peace of Magnolia

> Truly, I say to you, unless you turn and
> become like children, you will never enter the
> kingdom of heaven.
>
> —Mathew 18:1–3

I FEEL MYSELF lying on my back, still too groggy to open my eyes. My body feels heavy, bruised, and swollen—every joint stiff and aching. And worst of all, my chest feels tight again, like there's something very heavy setting on top of it.

Finally, I will myself to open my eyes.

Looking up, I try to focus, seeing a blurry view of my son. I am happy to be back with him, of course, but I'm disappointed I'm back in this aging body and hospital room. I'm old, and I am ready for whatever lies ahead—as long as I can leave my pain behind. I've lived a long life, a lot of it with pain and heartache but, for the most part, a happy life. I just hope my son can be happy.

It's hard not to let it show. I try to disguise how sad I am to be back to reality, with a long list of physical and health limitations. When I try to breathe deeply, which a moment ago felt like a regular, effortless breath, I'm thrown immediately into a painful coughing spell. *Yes, I am definitely back to reality.*

"Hey, Mikey."

"Hi, Pop. It looked like you were breathing deeply and dreaming there for a while. You were also smiling in your sleep. Were you back in Magnolia?"

"I was—and oh, Mike, I was on my bike, my black Schwinn. I rode to Nick and John's and the bakery and ran over the bell-signal hoses at the Sinclair gas station." A smile returns to my face from merely thinking about my adventures, but it fades away as yet another coughing fit comes upon me. "I never made it to Bob's."

"It's all right, Pop. Just relax. Don't try to talk too much. I think the meds you are on are pretty strong. It's normal to experience these kinds of hallucinations."

"Yeah, you are probably right, but I've never had a more vivid dream." I pause to catch my breath. Mike nods sympathetically, the way somebody indulging a toddler who's convinced Santa Claus is real might.

With a forced smile, he holds a cup of water with a straw up to my lips, and I take a slow sip, wondering if there's a way to convince him this doesn't feel like just a drug-induced dream as much as it feels like traveling back in time.

It dawns on me that perhaps it doesn't matter. Of course I'm not actually traveling through time, and of course what I'm seeing isn't real—I just wish he could grasp how much it means to see these things again. To feel *alive* again. I want that for Mike.

"Did they give you lunch yet, Dad?"

As I try and think whether I ate or not, my mind keeps concentrating on the brownie, the Mallo Cup, and the cream soda. "Yes, I think I ate. I am still tasting the Mallo Cup."

"Mallo Cup?"

"From my dream. It was one of my favorite candies growing up. Crazy how I still taste it."

Mike looks at me with half a smirk. "Do you need anything else before I go? Water? Ice? Pain medicine?"

"No, I am fine, but can we talk for just a few moments before you go, Mike?"

"Of course we can, Pop."

"I know you have been through a lot in your life, Mike. Losing your brother and then losing Mom. It hasn't been easy for you, but I want you to know that I hope you are happy. You have a beautiful family, son, and there is no better gift you can give to them than to be happy. They will sense it and also be happy. That preacher fellow that was here when you left—he made a lotta sense to me."

"I am glad, Pop."

"Listen, Mike, I'm not going to be around much longer. I sense it. My wish for you is to experience faith and joy in your life. I don't want to preach, but I do know that faith will make life's unexpected events easier to deal with."

"Faith? Really, Pop? Even after what happened to Tim? Mom and you lost your faith after Tim, and look how brokenhearted Mom was. That eventually killed her. I am sure of it. And now I am supposed to have faith and be happy?"

"I know, son. It won't happen overnight. All I am asking is to open the door and let God slowly work on you. I don't think my visits to Magnolia are just dreams—I think I am close to the end, Mikey." Coughing interrupts me once again, but after I settle down, I continue. "I have a lot of regrets, and I know Timmy's death made me bitter, but somehow, I have always felt that God exists, despite the tragedies we've dealt with." Another, longer, coughing spell takes over.

"Don't worry about that, Pop. Listen, you've been a great father. I wish I spent more time with you. You'll get through this, and we will spend more time together. I promise."

"I don't know what's ahead for me, Mike. But I do know that more than anything else, I want you to be happy, and I am sure Mom and Tim want that too."

"I will try. Is that what you want to hear? Don't ask me how, but I promise I will try. I could sure use a sign to help me, though."

"I am relying heavily on God's mercy. If there is a heaven and if, by some miracle, I end up there, I promise I will try and let you know, but try and stay open minded."

Getting too weak to talk, I lean back on my pillow, calling Mike closer as I whisper to him, "Give the girls a hug for me, and buy them a Mallo Cup."

"I will, Pop. I'll try and bring them up tomorrow. You know teenagers and how they are always running."

"Yes, I do, but I would love to see them, Mike. Hey, don't forget our promises."

"I won't, Pop. You rest, and I will see you tomorrow."

I watch my son leave and wonder if I will ever see him again. I look up at the ceiling and think back to the vivid sights and sounds of my Magnolia visits. *I hope I can go back.* I rest, breathing shallowly to avoid a coughing spell and all the accompanying chest pain.

Slowly, I drift off. And for a while, I simply sleep.

But eventually, I find myself sitting on my bike, leaning against the wall of Bob's corner store, holding a small brown bag of penny candy. I must have already gone in and selected an assortment of them. Looking through the bag, I sample some.

I enjoy the candy and my pain-free, zestful state, purposely avoiding the urge to make sense of any of this. I decide to ride my bike back down Evesham Road to Albertson Park. By the time I get there, I am down to just two red JuJu Coins, which I toss into my mouth. These cherry-flavored coins are soft and chewy, but they stick to your teeth like crazy. *Hopefully, they won't bother my crowns.* I laugh as I slide my tongue to my back molars and remember that, of course, I don't have any crowns. I have perfect, healthy teeth.

While riding my bike through the park, I look at the giant sliding board, recalling the times my friends and I rubbed wax paper on the surface. When you climbed up—and it was a good climb—and sat at the top looking down, you knew you were about to launch yourself down and across the grass at supersonic speed. It was awesome.

Getting back on my bike and riding on, I recall Memorial Day in Magnolia and the parade, which started here at Albertson Park, ran down Evesham Road to Warwick Road, and ended at the American Legion next to Magnolia Public School. It was an amazing parade. In fact, I used to be in it when I was a Cub Scout. Now, some eighty years later, here I am, riding my bike through all this but in a dream. Ha!

Upon arriving at the Legion, I park my bike next to the World War II cannon, which looks the same as when I used to play on it. I remember the veterans who delivered a three-gun salute here during the Memorial Day commencement. There was always a thrill in picking up the empty shells when they finished. Then came the birch beer and hot dogs—plenty to go around. I can almost taste that juicy, flavorful hot dog and the crisp, carbonated tang of the birch beer as I look at the grade school I attended.

Suddenly, I think of Miss Pettengill—my fifth-grade teacher. She always kept our class under control, for sure. She was very stern, but I must say, I thought she was a great teacher. I hated math until I received her guidance. She turned me around. I was motivated to work hard and make her happy with my progress.

Magnolia Public School is next to the Legion, so I push off on my bike and ride up to the window of my fifth-grade class—Miss Pettengill's classroom. As I peer inside the windows, I recall the day I was handing out papers when the principal came in to inform the class that President John F. Kennedy had been shot. I guess I will never forget that day. Just before pulling away from the window, I see a figure moving inside the classroom. It's a woman sitting behind the teacher's desk.

What? Miss Pettengill? Oh my God! She looks the same as she did when I was in her class.

I cup my hands around my eyes and continue looking inside. Miss Pettengill looks up from her desk and smiles at me, causing me to panic and fall off my bike. Now, I know I am dreaming but still—that fall didn't even hurt. I get back on my bike and peer back into the classroom, seeing only a teacher's desk there now.

I laugh, shaking my head.

Whatever they're giving me in this IV is really doing its job, but I'm not going to complain; I'm enjoying every moment back here in Magnolia.

I leave the window and ride around to the back of the school, where there is a huge playground with monkey bars and the spinning rings.

Ah yes, the rings.

My favorite, and they seem intact. Dismounting my bike, I run and grab on to one of the rings, which is attached to a rope tethered to the top of a metal canopy. The rope can spin and rotate to follow wherever the ring takes it. As I run, the canopy turns—and the faster I run, the faster it turns. Eventually, I jump into the air, holding on tightly to the ring, and up I go, spinning high off the ground.

Like my time on the Tarzan rope, I am overcome by a feeling of exhilarating relief. I've forgotten what it's like to move my body this way, without pain or fear of injury. It's enough to bring tears to my eyes. I hold tightly to the ring and feel the wind in my face and the pull of gravity. Whenever my feet find the ground again, I run so fast that I achieve higher heights and faster falls.

I feel like I'm a kid again. *Am I . . . a kid again?*

My feet skid to a stop, and for a moment, the world goes quiet. I'm holding the ring in my hands, sneakers in the sand below me, overlooking a silent playground that, for the first time, feels slightly eerie. Outside the soft coo of a mourning dove and the general sound of traffic in the distance, I'm alone out here.

It's just a dream, I remind myself. *A dream I'm enjoying. Even though it isn't real, I'm happy to be a kid again. This doesn't need to be real . . . . The fact that it's a believable dream is enough for me.*

I take one more trip around the pole, swinging and flying into the air, before I find my feet thudding into the sand again and walking back to my bike. As I ride home, I hear the jingle of an ice cream truck creeping down Camden Avenue.

Oh, the ice cream cones I ate from that truck . . . and for only ten cents!

Occasionally, I'd get a pineapple sundae for thirty-five cents, and, on special occasions, I would get a banana boat for fifty-five cents. The banana boat was the Mister Softee version of a banana split. I recall how it was organized, but I am sure there were variations. The banana boat I remember had three twirls of custard—two vanilla twirls on the ends, one with fudge topping and one with cherry, and a chocolate twirl in the middle with pineapple topping. It also had, of course, a banana, split longways, a half on each side, all accented by whipped cream and a cherry on top.

I ride to the corner of the playground, stopping at the softball backstop almost out of sheer habit, after spending so many years lounging up there, eating candy. The mere thought of it brings a smile to my face.

Oh hell . . . why not?

I get off my bike and climb up the backstop, sitting there for a while, allowing myself to remember all the fun I had on this playground. I laugh, thinking about my friends and how we used to pick sticker burs and throw them on each other's clothing. Even during class. It was hysterical to see kids sitting in class, unaware they had sticker burs on their back and in their hair. I find myself laughing out loud at the memory.

As I lie back on the top of the backstop, looking up at the clouds, I think, *How is it that I have enjoyed three visits to Magnolia? Three trips back in time. Three trips that have reminded me of what it feels like to be really alive . . .*

As my son said, it's probably the drugs they are giving me.

As the clouds drift by, I think of all the places I have reexperienced over these three visits, absorbing all the joy and the freedom and the peace.

But despite all the positives, something haunts the back of my mind—and it took place today, during this visit.

The empty playground. Besides paying for the candy and the brownie, I have been entirely alone during every one of my visits to Magnolia.

When I was young, I had plenty of friends here, but I did spend a great deal of time alone: playing in the yard, climbing trees, fishing, riding my bike, building models like Frankenstein and Wolf Man, and, of course, watching TV.

Life was just . . . well, amazing growing up in Magnolia.

What was it? Was it the time? The freedom? The energy of youth?

The chain-link backstop pushes against my back. I roll my shoulders and say out loud, "I think it was the newness."

Everything was fresh, and there wasn't much thinking. I just lived day to day, taking in every experience and accepting it for what it was and nothing more—the smell of those small white roses, the flavor of that ripe peach, the texture of the rope as I climbed it, the sound of the birds. It's time to face the question I keep avoiding.

Why am I back here now?

Why, really, does this all feel so real?

I lean against the chain-link backstop, looking up at the clouds, and notice the sun isn't casting off the steady sheets of gold it normally does. *No, there's something strange about it. It's . . . flickering.*

I stand up straighter and realize I'm able to look at the sun directly.

That's not normal. Neither is the flickering.

To add to the strangeness, I begin to hear faint voices. "His pupils are very dilated," a voice says, followed by another saying, "His blood pressure is barely registering."

And suddenly, without warning, it's as though I can't take my eyes off that flickering sun, and everything around me begins fading away, replaced by a circle of masked faces looking down at me.

No longer am I relaxing on the chain-link backstop. And no longer is the sunlight flickering—what I'm really looking at is the doctor's flashlight. It appears I am coming back to reality again but straddling the line between the two lives: a life when I was twelve years old, without a care in a world, and a life when I'm ninety-two years old, with every reason not only to care but to be very afraid.

I feel myself crumble against the fear, shrinking away from it—and my life in Magnolia gets brighter as my life in the hospital begins to fade.

I'm not ready to face the plight of being ninety-two and possibly on my deathbed—not when there's still so much to love about life, to experience. Perhaps it makes me a bit of a coward, or perhaps it makes me human, but I block out the hospital and the doctors and the voices and the physical pain, allowing Magnolia to eclipse it all yet again.

A few moments pass, during which I continue to get flashes of light, voices, and the terrifying sensation of the inability to breathe, but I deliberately force myself to focus on what's in front of me: the oak tree swaying in a soft breeze, the spill of sunlight cast over my arms and shoulders like melted butter.

I'm home. I'm safe, I tell myself, squeezing my eyes shut. *I'm home now. I'm safe.*

Slowly, Magnolia returns to its original, undisturbed state, and I know I've blocked out the reality of the hospital, my failing health, and the doctors. Once again, I tell myself, *I'm home, I'm safe, and I can stay here for as long as I'd like.*

But the truth is, I'm not sure any of these things are true.

I have purposely not addressed why or how these visits to Magnolia are possible. I have just enjoyed them, presuming they'd be short-lived, drug-induced dreams. But now, even though I'm home and I'm safe, a deep sadness is creeping in. Why?

"This is my fourth visit here, and I know—" I pause, wondering if I'm even capable of admitting this out loud to myself. "These visits are more than dreams."

As though to emphasize my point, the world around me stays perfectly silent.

There isn't another person to be found, and I think this very well could be the root of the deep sadness I'm feeling now.

My eyes wander from the oak tree to the garden to the house itself, and I say aloud to myself and only to myself, "I've found your one imperfection, Magnolia—you aren't real."

When I lived here as a child, I experienced the Tarzan rope and cheap candy and fudgy brownies and ice cream trucks for the first time. Everything was fresh and new, stripped of the responsibilities of adulthood. I didn't have to think twice about my life as it unfolded—I just lived it.

When I was here as a kid, my family was close by, and I knew that no matter where I roamed, in and out of Magnolia—Albertson Park, Nick and John's, Bob's, the railroad tracks, fishing at Kirkwood Lake, climbing trees, delivering papers, or just daydreaming on top of the backstop—I had to be home at suppertime.

My family would all be together then. But they aren't all together now. And my current family isn't together either.

Yes, I am back home. I'm able to breathe deeply and move without pain. I'm back in the peace of Magnolia.

But this time, I am not alone.

CHAPTER 4

Where Am I?

> So valuable to heaven is the dignity of the human soul that every member of the human race has a guardian angel from the moment the person begins to be.
>
> —St. Jerome

ALTHOUGH GRATEFUL FOR these interludes away from the hospital and my frail condition, the difference is that this time—*this time*—I am profoundly alone. There is no suppertime or family to come home to. Just as I feel myself spiraling into a sense of desperate loneliness, I hear a voice.

"You are not alone, Lou."

I look around, and from behind the pink dogwood tree emerges a man. He has dark brown hair, an average build, and strong facial features with piercing blue eyes. I sense a calmness about him. He approaches me with a gentle smile. "Beautiful day here in Magnolia, huh, Lou?"

I study him as he gets closer. He's familiar, somehow, but I can't really place where I know him from. "Do I know you?"

Smiling, he replies, "Not as well as I know you."

"Well, yes, I sense that—but for the life of me, I do not remember you."

"I didn't expect you to know me, Lou, but I have known you for some time. In fact, I have been by your side your entire life."

I laugh, unable to hide my skepticism. "By my side my entire life? Who are you—my guardian angel?"

He looks at me with his deep blue eyes and smiles. "I am. My name is Micah. I was assigned to you, Louis—from the time you were conceived all the way up to this point now. I'll be your guardian beyond now too."

"Wait, you said *beyond*? As in beyond life?"

Micah smiles, nodding. "Yes, but I wouldn't call it 'beyond life.' It's more like beyond the life you knew." Micah sits down across from me on the bench and watches the rays of sun dancing on my arms and all around on the picnic table. "Feels good here in Magnolia, doesn't it, Lou? You like the warmth of the sun?"

"Yeah, it feels pretty good . . . . Micah, I'm not quite sure why I am here now—well, scratch that, actually, I have no clue why I am here." We both laugh a little but only for a few breaths; then everything returns to something slightly more serious. "Why am I here in Magnolia, in the yard I grew up in?"

He furrows his brows. "Do you not like being back in Magnolia?"

"Of course I do," I say promptly. "I just . . . Magnolia is so much better than lying in a hospital bed, unable to string a sentence together without coughing, but I just am not sure why I've been sent here, specifically."

Micah smiles with a deep intensity in his eyes. It's almost as though he's looking right through me, or he's rehearsed and dreaded this very moment. "I am very much aware of your hospital situation, Lou."

"Oh yes, I guess you would be if you were my guardian angel, wouldn't you?"

"You sound skeptical."

"Well, how am I supposed to sound? For one thing, I thought angels were spirits and couldn't be seen with physical eyes, but here you are in Magnolia, sitting with me at this picnic table." I pause, and Micah continues to study me in a way that somehow reminds me of Mike. It's the look family gives you when they've got bad news they're afraid to share. "Apparently you have names," I say, trying to keep things light.

"We do, indeed," answers Micah.

I look closely at him, sitting across from me at the picnic table, feeling both settled and unsettled. Settled in that he has such a peace about him but unsettled because the presence of an angel raises questions. *Why here? Why now?*

And another question, of course, that I'm not ready to ask yet.

"And where are your wings?"

"Angels do not have wings. Artists, way back in the fourth century, depicted angels with wings, and, well, it stuck." He shrugs. "But no. We don't have wings. You'll learn more about angels soon, though, Lou. Your questions will be answered."

"I will learn more about angels? What exactly do you mean by that, Micah?"

Micah continues in a soothing, trustworthy voice as he reaches over to hold my arm. "As I said, Lou, guardian angels can materialize when it's appropriate. I materialized as a chaplain very recently in your hospital room."

"Frank?"

"Yes, and I materialized for you years ago when you lost your son in that terrible accident."

The mere mention of Tim's death brings tears to my eyes. Looking up at Micah, I ask him directly, "Where was Tim's guardian angel that day?"

Micah looked as though he expected this question. "God has never promised that we'll never get hurt or sick or have other problems in life, Lou. But he *has* promised to be with us when hard times come—and one way he does this is through his angels. That was a hard time for your family. No parent should have to go through what you did. The earthly realm is not heaven, my friend. You will come to understand this more than ever now that your capacity to understand such things is unlimited."

I study Micah's face. Is he just a figment of this drug-induced dream, like everything else I've experienced here? Part of me worries that's what's going on while another part of me desperately wants this to be real.

"You said you appeared to me during that time?" I go on, figuring I'll ask all the questions I like. I've got nothing to lose.

"I did," he says. "I visited in various forms, but it was very difficult for you to notice me. Then, thirty years ago, when you lost your wife. And then shortly after, when you were recovering from open-heart surgery, I visited you in the form of a nurse, remember?"

"I do remember a nurse who comforted me and gave me such hope as I lay there in pain, missing my son and wife more than ever." Gazing up into the big oak tree as the flicker of sunlight warms me, I think back twenty years, to that quadruple bypass operation. "Oh, the pain—especially if I had to cough or, God forbid, sneeze."

"I always wondered why I never saw that nurse after that day she visited me. Are you saying that was you? I thought that nurse seemed like she knew me, and she was so compassionate and so empathetic."

"You needed that to give you some sense of hope, Lou." After a few moments, Micah, still grasping my arm, looked into my eyes. "The other time we always materialize is when the person we are assigned to passes away."

As Micah's words sink in, my mood shifts. Suddenly, despite the sunlight's warmth, I feel very cold. My eyes sting with tears, and I think of looking up at the doctor's flashlight only moments ago and willing myself out of that hospital room and back here.

Back to Magnolia.

The gravity of what I've done strikes like a thunderclap.

I look at Micah, who continues to grasp my arm. "Did I die, Micah?"

Nodding and tightening his grasp on me, Micah answers me directly. "You passed from the earthly realm to the spiritual realm, but you are not dead. You lived an amazing life, ninety-two years' worth of experiences, relationships, and adventures. You had your share of ups and downs, for sure, but truly, you had an amazing life. It was a pleasure guiding you as I think back and count all the odds you've beaten, people you've loved, and joys you've experienced in your life."

I try frantically to make sense of all this. *Am I still dreaming? Is this becoming a nightmare?*

"I've been with you from the beginning, Lou." Micah looks around the yard with as much fondness as I do. "All the experiences here in Magnolia and beyond. I was always next to you as you rode your bike." He circled his hand around me, as if he was gesturing across my lifetime. "Always with you when you drove your '54 Chevy and your Jeep and your Hondas.

And I was also with you recently when you were on the school playground lying on that backstop, wondering about your visits here to Magnolia while slowly realizing what made growing up here so magical."

So many things run through my mind. *I passed? What does that even mean? Where am I? Is this heaven? Where is everyone? I don't deserve to be here.*

It's like Micah heard my questions loud and clear. "Yes, I told you, you passed, Lou. You will begin to know exactly what that means. I will be guiding you on a journey—a journey on a path that leads to heaven. Where is everyone? They're here, and you will meet them all."

My emotions get the best of me as Micah's words sink in. I break down crying and, not knowing what else to do, I hug Micah. "I never thought heaven was real or that I would go there." I continue sobbing as I lift my head up and look around. "So my recent visits here to Magnolia while I was in the hospital . . . they were *your* doing?"

"Yes, Lou. I wanted you to regain some of the feelings and experiences you had at the point in your life when you were most free, most real, and most your true self."

"My true self was a boy riding my bike, eating candy, playing on the trains, and swinging on my Tarzan rope?"

"I know it sounds odd, but yes. What did God say? 'Unless you turn and become like children, you will not enter the kingdom of heaven.' So I brought you to the place where you were most free, a time when there was no thinking or rationalizing, no heavy decisions. Well, *almost*," he adds, giving me something of a smirk. "You still had to decide whether to buy a Clark bar or a pack of baseball cards. Remember when you found an empty soda bottle and redeemed it at Nick and John's for a nickel?"

I manage to smile through my tears as Micah recounts that crucial decision, then become more serious. "You didn't address my last thought."

"You mean whether you deserve to be here?"

"Yes. My bitterness and disbelief, my turning away from God, all my years of doubt? I am worthy of heaven?"

"The answer to that question is easy. No one is worthy of heaven, and as far as your true self goes, it shined brightest in Magnolia in that you experienced life with a real and fresh outlook, free from all the pressures of life, free from the fear of judgment. And free from bitterness. You simply took life in. The smell of those white roses, the feel of Japanese beetles in your hand, the taste of freshly picked blackberries, walking in the parade, having a hot dog and birch beer, burning the leaves, picking tomatoes—need I go on? I am not condoning the lack of thought for many of the actions you took during that time, like jumping from boxcar to boxcar on the railroad tracks or running through the drainage pipes. I am saying you just lived life. Not only were you your true self growing up here in Magnolia, but you were also very close to heaven."

"Close to heaven? Well, I would have never made that connection, but I'll take an angel's word for it," I say with a half laugh. "I am sure I will come to understand this more fully as we go through . . . well, as we go through our time together, I suppose."

Micah nods. "Yes, you will understand a great deal as we progress, Lou. You will understand things you could never understand when you were in the earthly realm." Micah reaches out and gently holds my arm again, conveying a deep sense of comfort and peace as he says, "I know you are shocked and confused and full of questions. That is normal and to be expected, and I will answer all of them. We will be in this together as you progress through various stages of heaven and come to learn about so many things—things you can't even imagine at this point. That's why I said you will learn everything you want to about angels. In fact, you will learn everything about anything you want to, whenever you want to."

As Micah is speaking, I know he is right about one thing: I *am* shocked and confused but also amazed and sad. Amazed this is happening but sad I left Mike and his family behind. Also, the sadness I felt on the backstop suddenly comes rushing back to me. *I will miss it here in Magnolia.*

"I feel your sadness, Lou," Micah says, "but trust me, your family is fine—and once you get a glimpse of what is ahead for you and them, there will be no more sadness, believe me. Let me just say this: the joy and peace you experienced in your childhood here in Magnolia, the love you experienced with your family, and all the joy you experienced throughout your life, all of it—it's but a speck of the total joy ahead of you."

As Micah comforts me, I start to relax. The profound joy I've felt during my life, and even now, during my visits to Magnolia, has been so substantial that it feels terrifying and devastating to leave it behind. But if Micah's right and it represents a mere speck of what's to come?

Well, I'm excited for that.

I look down at my arms and don't see all those ugly age spots anymore. My silver hair is gone. I ponder this forecast of joy. It is . . . well, it is invigorating. Invigorating? Hell, I haven't been invigorated in some time. Micah's sincerity makes me feel like I've known him all my life—and I guess, in a way, I have.

"You mentioned my '54 Chevy. Was that you who—"

"Was that me who saved you from that head-on collision?" Micah interrupts. "Yes, it was me. Your reflexes were somewhat diminished that night. Why?"

"Ah yes." I sigh. "We had been drinking back behind Camden County College."

"Indeed, you had been."

"And my Beetle? The day I was installing my eight-track tape player?"

"You mean the day you almost drilled into the gas tank?"

Laughing at my past stupidities that had almost gotten me killed, I commented, "I always tell people that story. I never knew what made me stop and see what that metal object I was hitting with the drill bit was. Duh! Yes, the Beetle's gas tank was in the front of the car—right where my head was while I was drilling to mount the eight-track player. But now I know. What were you doing? Yelling in my ear 'Stop!' or something?"

Micah smiled. "For the most part, yes."

"I guess I kept you pretty busy over my lifetime."

"You did, but I didn't expect anything less. You were active all through your life—yes, playing on the trains, climbing trees, walking through the drainage pipes of Magnolia, riding your bike just about everywhere, including your many fishing excursions from one lake to another, playing on the ice on Laurel Lake . . . . Remember that day with your cousin Anthony?"

"I do. That was scary. We didn't belong on that ice—" Then, suddenly, it dawns on me that Anthony, who died fairly young, would hopefully be in heaven now. "Hey, will I see Anthony? I mean, now that I am . . . well, here?" And before I give Micah a chance to respond, my mind shifts to my son who died so tragically and so young. "And, for that matter, will I see my Timmy?"

I could have asked if I would see my wife, Jill, or my parents, for I missed them all, but Timmy's death changed my whole life and our family's life, and I've carried such an emptiness with me since he died. I have always wanted to know if he was safe and at peace.

"Of course you will, Lou. You will embrace your son and wife again and all your family and friends, but give it time. We are just beginning our journey."

The thought of seeing and embracing Timmy and Jill again sends something that can only be described as warm vibrations through my body. With those vibrations come such a release—a release of years of bitterness. The vibrations are replaced by a desperate sort of enthusiasm, however, which prompts me to ask, "How long will this journey take?"

"The concept of time as you know it, and as you've always known it, will change drastically, my friend. Time passes, yes, but not time as you are used to measuring it."

CHAPTER 5

Welcome to the Spiritual Realm

> What the caterpillar calls the end of the
> world the master calls a butterfly.
> —Richard Bach

MICAH SMILES AT me. "So, are you ready for this journey, Lou?"

"Now? Today?"

"Yes, now. Why? Are you tired? Do you need a nap?"

I squint up at the large oak tree's canopy, the sunlight sparkling through the tapestry of leaves. "No, I feel great. I have never felt better." I process his suggestion of taking a nap and scoff. "And a nap? Being tired? Will I get tired here? Will I sleep here? Are there days and nights here?"

"Wow, Lou, these are very good questions and a great place for us to start." Micah sits back in his seat, peering up at the canopy the way I was moments ago, before letting his blue eyes find mine again. "Let's start with sleep. For your last ninety-two years, sleep was a physical necessity for your earthly body. Without it, your brain would've stopped working correctly, and your body would have refused to cooperate. The sleep-wake cycle is just another of the many patterns God has put into place on the earth."

"One of many?"

"There are many cycles that are a part of life on earth—day and night, the change of the seasons, annual animal migrations, the growing and harvesting of crops, the flow of water from evaporation to precipitation, and many more. But you are no longer part of those cycles, my friend. You are in a different realm. You can still sleep here or take a nap, but you really don't need to. You have probably noticed all the energy you have."

"I noticed that on my first visit to Magnolia—so much energy. I didn't think about it much. I didn't want to. I just wanted to enjoy not being in pain or coughing, but yes, the tremendous energy. I felt like a kid again. I feel that way now. No, I don't need a nap."

Micah's smile gets even brighter. "I'm sure you feel tremendous energy, Lou, but I assure you, the energy is just the beginning. You will have unlimited energy and unlimited time to accomplish unimaginable things. As far as day and night here? Let's just say that at this point, in this first dimension of heaven, yes, there are still day and night, like the earth you are familiar with."

"First dimension," I say, intrigued. "Okay, I guess that dimension thing will be understood as I go. So, then, there are still sunrises and sunsets?"

"Yes. Don't worry, Lou, you will learn more about this later as your journey unfolds."

MAGNOLIA

I take some time to absorb what Micah is telling me, but he clearly senses my mind racing. He asks me, "What's on your mind, Lou? I know it's a lot to take in, especially in the beginning."

"I was just thinking . . . . Well, I should be so happy to be here. Here on this journey with you, all that. But I am also wondering how I ever made it here."

"What do you mean?"

"I am just thinking perhaps I don't deserve to be here. I look back over my life, and, well . . . I guess I could have been a better person. After Jill died, I rarely went to church, and, to be totally honest, much of my bitterness grew from being mad at God."

Micah nods. "I understand, Lou. This may surprise you, but no one *deserves* to be here. Consider it a gift from God."

"Why would God give me such a gift? I ignored him most of my life. I was selfish. I wasn't too generous, and I did a lot of bad things."

"A lot of bad things? Name some."

"Well, surely you know about the time I threw that box turtle as high as I could and let it fall down onto the street." I shake my head, horrified. "God, I can't believe I did that."

"That was pretty bad, but you were a kid, and if I'm not mistaken, you have agonized about that event throughout your life."

"Yeah, but I should have known better. How could I have done that?"

"How many turtles did you torture, Lou?"

"Just the one, and yes, I did regret that I had such a total disregard for life."

"If you had done that to multiple turtles over time or if you had never regretted it, there might have been a problem, but, as you've said, you've felt remorse for that event often."

"How about the time my friends and I stole clotheslines from across the neighborhood and tied Mr. Simmons's house up with them so he couldn't get out, and then we threw eggs at his house?"

At this, Micah laughed hysterically. "Yes, I remember, and I remember the night Mr. Simmons almost caught you as you and your friends ran down Camden Avenue."

I laugh as well. "Yeah, he was gaining on me. He was so close, I heard him breathing just behind me, then I shifted into high gear and passed my friends like they were standing still."

"Yes, you were fast," After we have a good laugh, Micah adds, "But yes, you enjoyed your childhood, and yes, you may have done a few bad things, but you turned out all right. As you grew into a man, you accepted the responsibility of a job and family, and you were always appreciative of all your blessings. What else lingers on your mind that makes you feel unworthy to be on this journey?"

I look down at the table. "Well, throughout my life, I guess I did a lot of bad things."

"And a lot of good things as well. I won't list them, but let's just say the good things outweighed the bad things many times over. Remember, I was with you all those years. We've often talked about how kind, empathetic, and appreciative you were in your life. Remember when your friend Bobby didn't have money for a hoagie at Nick and John's? You gave him half of yours. I only mention that event because you were thinking about when you were young, here in Magnolia. But throughout your life, Lou, you kept an open heart, and, as I said, you acknowledged God for all his blessings, big and small. I disagree about you not being generous and that you ignored God. You were very generous with your time, talents, and treasure."

"Time, talents, and treasure?"

"You made time for people. Not just your family and friends, but everyone you encountered. You freely shared your knowledge and experience. You recommended doctors, restaurants, books, movies, and services. You loved seeing people happy. And that, my friend, is not ignoring God. He loves all his creations, especially his human creations, and he is very much aware of how you loved them as well."

"Well, thank you, Micah. Maybe I wasn't so bad after all. You said, 'We've often talked' a moment ago. Who's we?"

"We angels communicate," he says, grinning. "And, as I mentioned, we are also in communication with God—as you are too, but we are just more aware of it. You too will become very aware of it soon enough."

I gaze at Micah as he interjects that small detail about the awareness of God. I want to ask more about God but decide to believe him that I will be aware of it soon enough. For now, I'll be patient.

"How much intervention does a guardian angel even have?" I ask. "Did you try and keep me on the right road, or did I have the free will to go in whichever direction I wanted?"

"We guardian angels cannot oblige people to follow the path of goodness. We cannot make decisions for you. You had complete free will throughout your life. Our only influence is one of support during challenging times."

"I'm happy to hear I did have free will." I laugh, still in shock over all this.

"Yes, God gives humans the opportunity to make choices that affect their destiny. He created mankind in his own image, and that includes the ability to choose. However, free will does not mean you can do anything you please. You can't jump off a bridge and fly. In addition to those natural limitations, he gave you the responsibility to choose wisely. And you are here, Lou, because of most of those choices, especially the ones that involved loving those around you."

"So I was free to ignore the intuition to stop drilling underneath the dashboard of my VW and not check what my drill bit was hitting?"

"Oh, of course," Micah says with a nonchalant shrug. "In fact, most people ignore their intuition altogether. It was my job to observe and support you—not shepherd or direct you."

"And yet, I got the feeling to stop drilling," I say, a bit confused. "And you gave me that feeling, right?"

"We're connected, you and I," Micah explains thoughtfully, and I realize there is a lot of nuances to this subject that may still go over my head. "Sometimes it's possible to tap into your angel's emotional profile. I was worried for your well being, and you tapped into that worry, producing the essence of intuition."

"That's . . ." I shake my head, amazed. "That's wonderful. What else do you do?"

"Many things," Micah says. "Again, all of which you'll learn about soon enough."

"And how does God fit into all this?"

"God *is* all this."

"I always felt there was a God," I say, smiling. "So many times, I tried to learn more about him, and at times I thought I was making progress—but then, inevitably, I always seemed to return to a state where doubt crept in."

"I understand. You had an active life—a family, job, house, friends, et cetera, et cetera. You were not alone in that respect, Lou. But you were sincere in your efforts: the books you read, the movies you watched, the churches you attended, and the way you prayed. Praying was key because it affirmed your belief in God, but you didn't just say the words; you lived your life accordingly, treating people with respect and love—both those you loved and those you didn't even know."

"Well, Micah, I appreciate that. I must say, I am glad to be here with you, as opposed to, well, the alternative place."

Micah chuckles. "The alternative place? Interesting way of putting it. What exactly are you referring to?"

"You know," I say, awkwardly. "Hell."

"To be in hell is to be on the wrong path," Micah says, looking intensely in my eyes for a moment. "It is hard to understand now—but again, in time, you will understand everything about this."

I breathe deeply as Micah describes hell—a place I've always believed was a literal location created by God to punish the sinful. The thought of not being on this path—the right path—is mind boggling. My understanding and awareness are limited, of course, but the assurance that they will expand, along with the promise of being reunited with my family, is a feeling that no words can describe. It's like that first sip of a vanilla milkshake from Nick and John's—so good, with so much more to come. But at the same time, I am thinking about those who never got that first sip.

As usual, Micah senses my uneasiness. "You are concerned," he says. "What about?"

"I was just thinking about those who died young, before discovering prayer or even having had a chance to do good things in their life. For that matter, how about those who were never born?"

"As I mentioned before, Lou, your concern for others is one of the main reasons you are on this path. The world is not heaven, and there is more than enough pain, death, and suffering to go around. As we move forward, the reasons for such pain and suffering will become clearer to you, but to your concern, those who died young and those who were never born, well.... Their journey to that ultimate and complete joy is much shorter."

I have so many questions about life and death, heaven and earth, and the path I am currently on. I also know that Micah always tries to answer my questions relative to my level of understanding, which is only growing as I proceed on my journey.

"Does everyone begin their spiritual journey from their hometown?" I ask.

With a slight chuckle, Micah tells me, "One's spiritual journey begins long before passing away, Lou, but no—not everyone has the same journey. That depends on their life and how they lived it. Your childhood in Magnolia was amazing, but not everyone had such a great childhood. For some, the freedom you experienced as a child happened much later in their life, and others never had that freedom at all. Ever."

We pause, entrenched in the gravity of his statement.

"Through no fault of their own," I say, and Micah's eyes sparkle.

"Everyone is different," he says simply. "For you, Magnolia was the perfect place for us to meet and begin this next chapter in your eternal life. You have to agree, you felt the freest during your childhood in Magnolia."

"Oh yes! I was so free during those days in Magnolia. It was simply amazing. I've always thanked God for that special time."

"That's normal, Lou. So many things in life can chip away at your sense of freedom. As you grew, you had to deal with responsibilities, schedules, commitments, and obligations. Then, as more time passed, you experienced regrets and resentments. They can bind your thoughts and constrict your heart, making you feel trapped in the past and anxious about the future. That energy you've been feeling here? It will become stronger as we transition your focus from the earthy realm to the spiritual realm. Eventually, Lou, you will touch the presence and peace of God and perceive the timelessness of divine life. There will be no past and no future. You will learn that in the present moment, you are free the way you were in those early years in Magnolia, but even more so."

I know this sounds incredible, but it has always been my nature to think that when things sound too good to be true, they usually are. But I also know that the playing field has changed considerably. As Micah said, I have transitioned from the earthly realm to the spiritual realm, and my thinking will eventually change as well, but for now, I express my concern to him. "I hope my journey will be successful, Micah. I hope I don't disappoint you. I mean, I will try to follow you and understand as we go, but it's a lot."

"Of course it's a lot, Lou, but we are not restricted to a school semester or the limits of an eight-hour workday. Just as you felt your energy level rise considerably, you will feel the level of your understanding rise as well. Trust me. It already has. Think back to before you went into the hospital—how were your thinking and speaking abilities?"

I nod to Micah's point. "They weren't good. Even simple words would not come to me, and I struggled to fit into a conversation, but you're right. I feel extremely clearheaded here."

As I look at Micah's face, I notice it's much lighter than when I first met him. In fact, it's almost illuminated. "Your face looks radiant, Micah."

"Radiant? Well, thank you. Remember when you asked where the light here comes from?"

"I do, and I am still curious about that."

"The light is within us, Lou. Our inner light reflects peace, goodness, and the light of God. Together we are luminous, shining bright and dispelling any darkness. You say I look radiant. Well, so are you." I reach up to feel my face, and Micah pulls out a handheld mirror from . . . well, from who knows, but he hands it to me. "Take a look."

As I hold the mirror up to my face, I am awestruck to see that it's partially illuminated. I look to Micah with an expression that begs for an explanation.

He acknowledges my surprise with a nod. "Welcome to the spiritual realm, Lou."

I shake my head in disbelief. "Are you sure this isn't a dream?"

"Not a dream, my friend. A gift—a gift that, as you mentioned, you don't deserve but, nonetheless, a gift from God. It's a gift that will expand your imagination as we continue on our journey together."

"I never considered my imagination to be anything more than fancy thoughts that had no real basis in reality."

"Well, that's true in some cases. They are just fancy thoughts, but sometimes, imagination changes into visualization and then to reality. Think about the Wright brothers. They *imagined* flying, and at first, that was just a thought. Then they started to visualize all aspects of it, and finally, they made it a reality."

"Yeah, I guess dreams are a lot like that—and the more I think about it, an artist probably imagines and visualizes a picture before they paint it."

"Great example. You could say that imagination is the ability of the mind to think in pictures, whether you are dreaming, daydreaming, planning, remembering, or meditating. And as active as anyone's imagination can be in the earthly realm, it can't hold a candle to what they can imagine in the spiritual realm. What was it Hamlet said to his friend? 'There are more things in heaven and earth, Horatio, than are dreamt of in your philosophy.' He was suggesting that the human imagination is limited, and there are many things we don't know—things that haven't been discovered and things we haven't even dreamed of. But more than that, Lou, the distinction between reality and imagination is going to change considerably here in the spiritual realm. As we progress, your reality will change—more than just your radiant appearance. Your imagination and visualization skills will increase and become resources for you and, eventually, a way of life here."

"Resources? You mean like tools?"

"Exactly. And, like any tool, you have to learn the proper way to use it. Remember when you were on the backstop, pondering what was missing from Magnolia?"

"Yes, I was thinking about—or visualizing, I guess—my family coming together at suppertime." I gesture over my shoulder, toward the back of my house. "Right there in the knotty-pine kitchen my dad built."

Micah reaches out his hands across the picnic table. "Hold my hands, close your eyes, and visualize a typical suppertime in that kitchen."

"You mean like when I was a boy?"

"Yes, that's fine. Try it."

Closing my eyes, I hold Micah's hands, slowly visualizing myself sitting at my place at the yellow Formica table. My dad is sitting at the head of the table to my left, always in his sleeveless T-shirt and usually with a tan from working outside so much. He was an outstanding carpenter. Across from me and next to my dad is my sister Linda. She always had a pleasant smile. Next to Linda is my oldest sister, Angela. I remember her glasses and how she and Linda always bickered with each other. To my right is my sister Marie, whom we all called Cheeks. I'm not sure how she got that nickname—probably because she had rosy cheeks. She was the closest to me in age; I was the youngest and the only boy. Across from my dad, at the other end of the table, is my mom. My mom was a great cook. Oh, the meals she made—veal cutlet, macaroni, and meatballs with an amazing red gravy, or sauce as the Medigans called it. (Back in the day, we referred to anyone who was not Italian as a Medigan.) And always a nice Jersey tomato and cucumber salad with vinegar and oil in the summertime.

As I visualize the table, the food, and everyone around it, I feel Micah squeeze my hands and say, "Now look at your mom more closely, Lou."

I smile but keep my eyes closed and try to imagine my mom in more detail. I see her walking back and forth from the oven to the table, wearing a housedress with an apron around her. Her hair is a reddish-brown color—maybe auburn is the correct word for it—and she kept it up with a kerchief. She has a pleasant smile. It makes her happy, seeing everyone at the table enjoying her dinner. As I look at her, she turns and smiles at me as if I am still a child, sitting there right now in real time. It feels so real. *She* feels so real.

It's as though everything else in this scene falls away, and I remain captivated by my mom. She looks like I can reach out and touch her. She's so young and beautiful and so full of life. Gazing at her, I forget where I am as our eyes meet, and I can't hold myself back from saying aloud, "Mom?"

"I am here, Louie."

The sound of her voice startles me, causing me to jump and open my eyes. Instead of gazing at my mother, I am staring at Micah "Oh my Gaw—*goodness!*"

Micah, still holding my hands and smiling at me, says, "Pretty real, huh, Lou?"

I just exhale. "Whew!" And then, after a pause, I tack on, "Soooo real."

Micah nods and continues. "That's just a small slice of the power of visualization, my friend. It will continue to grow, and, as I said, it will become a way of life for you."

"Well, *life* is a good word. I certainly don't care for the alternative. And *eternal life* is even better. I'm just not used to using my imagination or visualization like this, Micah. I guess I've always been—I don't know—more real or logical."

Micah, smiling and nodding in agreement, adds, "Albert Einstein said, 'Logic will get you from A to B, but imagination will take you everywhere.' That will be a major theme here, Lou."

As I hear Micah trying to explain the power of imagination, I am still fixated on my recent encounter with my mom. "I called out to her, Micah, and she told me she was here."

Micah looked at me again, with that look that penetrates my very soul, and says, "She *is* here, Lou, and you will see more of her."

As Micah tells me this, I can't hold back my tears. I start sobbing uncontrollably, like a baby. The encounter was real, and it shook my existence. *I've never cried like this!* I am overwhelmed by a sense of joy. The tears just keep flowing as I hold Micah's hands and gaze into his eyes.

"The joy you are feeling now, Lou, is just the tip of the iceberg."

CHAPTER 6

Fruits of the Spirit

> The fruit of the Spirit wasn't intended to be a
> list of goals for us to produce—it is the Holy
> Spirit through us who produces fruit.
>
> —Dan Kimball

I CIRCLE MY arm around. "So, all this—it's all real?"

"Oh, it's real, all right—just like you and I are real, and just like your mom was real, and just like Miss Pettengill was real." As I start to react, Micah adds, "And just like that chocolate brownie was real."

I smile, slapping my hand on the table. "I *knew* that brownie was real. I guess I am still confused between real and imaginary."

"You are expected to be confused in the beginning, my friend. That's because of your current understanding of what's physical and what's spiritual."

"I thought I had a decent understanding of them, for the most part."

"You did. You had the understanding that you were expected to have. A lot of things influenced you—family, friends, school, work, TV, books, and so forth. But now, we have a lot of rethinking to do."

I nod to indicate that I understand this, but the reality is I'm still a little shaky on it.

"How do I start to rethink these things, Micah?"

"Let's start with reality. The idea of bringing things to reality from your imagination is not something new. You've done this many times."

Looking at Micah, surprised, I say, "I did?"

"Yes, think back to when you really wanted something. Perhaps it started with an idea, but then it began to grow. Day after day, gradually, you started to think about it more and more, taking an idea and drawing it into your reality by acting on it. Planning to take a vacation or ask for a promotion or even to propose marriage—all those things started as an idea, as a vision. Then, through action, they became your reality."

I shake my head in awe. "So, are you saying I've always had this power?"

"Yes. You were just not aware of it." Micah pauses, giving me a smile. "People in the physical, earthly plane often forget the power of visualization—they are more compelled by the tangible."

"Are there any limits to visualization here?" I gesture to the oak tree, Magnolia—this heavenly space. "I mean, I know while I was alive, I was capable of this to a certain extent, but now that I'm here, is it possible for me to imagine *anything* and bring it to life by visualizing it?"

"Like you visualized that brownie and then ate it?"

"Ha! Yes, like that brownie."

"The turnaround time from visualization to realization is much faster here, Lou—as you might've noticed while envisioning your mom moments ago. Eventually, it will become instantaneous. You'll think of something you'd like, and it will instantly manifest."

"Well, I did that a lot in my lifetime, Micah, especially with food and especially with desserts. My visualizations made my mouth water."

We both laugh at that, and then I ask, "So, back to my question: Are my visualizations limited? Can I visualize my mom anytime I want and make her real?"

"Eventually, yes. But there is a limit. Your visualizations have to be compatible with the Spirit."

"The spirit? Whose spirit?"

"When we talk about the Spirit, Lou, we are talking about God. Here, we all strive to grow in spirit, and as we do, we can feel and know his Spirit. Everything draws from that Spirit—it creates and sustains all life, including eternal life. It inspires and equips us with abilities and gifts, and it guides us according to his will. Guardian angels like me are channels of that guidance. So when you ask me if your visualizations have limits, the answer is no, as long as they are in alignment with the fruits of the Spirit."

"Fruits of the Spirit? What are they?"

"Examples include love, joy, peace, kindness, goodness, consideration, faithfulness, and gentleness. Quite a view of God, wouldn't you say, Lou?"

As Micah is laying this out, my tears start to flow again. Everything I've learned so far flows over me like a wave of refreshing coolness. I breathe in deeply, embracing a joy more profound than I have ever felt before. The desire to thank God comes over me as I think to myself, *I am on a path to heaven, and I thank you, God, for putting me on this path with Micah. From my heart, Lord, I know I don't deserve it, but here I am. I will never go against your Spirit, and I hope you know how appreciative I am.*

Micah smiles and nods. "He knows."

Wiping my tears away, I tell him, "I promised Mike I would let him know if I ever made it to heaven."

"We will talk about that later, Lou, but you will have that opportunity."

"Oh, that will be so great. I want him to be happy in his life."

"Well, your talk with him went a long way, Lou. Trust me on that."

"Really? I wish I talked with him more. I wish I shared my thoughts with him more. Why do we always learn these things when it's too late?"

"It's not too late, Lou. As I said, your talk might not have seemed like much to you, but it went a long way, and you will see that."

Just knowing that makes me feel so . . . so full of joy. "So, getting back to my visualizations. You said they have to be compatible with the Spirit of God, which encompasses all those things. How will I know if what I am visualizing embodies that compatibility?"

"It's not hard, Lou. Think of them as simply being compatible with love. If they're compatible with love, then they are compatible with the Spirit of God."

"Can you give me an example?"

Micah smiles. "Sure. In the earthly realm, many people visualize wealth but go about seeking and obtaining it without compassion for their fellow man. Their wealth increases, but their charity does not. Or they may seek a better position, but in obtaining it, they disregard or mistreat others now that they are in a position of more authority. In both situations, their vision of happiness was never realized."

"So you're saying that if those visualizations included some of the fruits of the Spirit—such as kindness, goodness, and consideration—their visualizations would have been realized?"

"Yes, and to your question about limits—other than going against the Spirit, there are none."

I continue to nod as my mind drifts, thinking about what I can and can't bring to life through my new powers of visualization. "Can I visualize someone still in the earthly realm?"

"Like your son Mike?"

"You are good at this mind reading thing, but yes, like Mike. I guess I am anxious to share this."

"There are ways to contact people on earth but not through the visualization technique we have discussed. It's more through prayer. I will help you with that later on in your journey."

I remember many discussions with people asking or wondering whether they will see their pets in heaven. As I think about it, I can't really see anything that goes against the Spirit in that regard, and my mind drifts to Emma, our golden retriever from so many years ago. As I think about her, I ask myself, *Can I imagine Emma? Can I bring her to life by simply visualizing her alive? Surely this visualization is compatible with love.*

My mind drifts to an earlier time when I would come home from work and act like Emma was a lion, and she was attacking me. We would wrestle on the lawn or in the living room, and I would yell, "Killer lion!" As we wrestled, she would clamp her teeth around my arm but never bear down. I would pull her head into my face and act like I had her in some type of wrestling half nelson, but in reality, I was getting my hugs in, breathing in her soft golden hair and dog dander as she was biting my arm, pretending to tear me apart—when really, she wouldn't hurt a fly. I *loved* that dog.

Micah is apparently tapping into what I'm envisioning. He offers me a smile under those bright blue eyes of his and says, "What was it you used to tell people you wanted to do if you ever got to heaven?"

My first thought is, *How can he know about that?* but then I remember he's been with me my whole life. He must know everything about me. Still,

I'm not totally sure what he is referring to, and so I ask him, "You mean about the lion?"

"Yes. What was it you said? 'When I get to heaven, I want to wrestle a lion.'"

"Well, yeah, I've had that vision—but of course, I didn't mean that so literally. If I'm in heaven, I can't die, right? So, naturally, I thought I'd wrestle with a lion, but we wouldn't actually hurt each other. We'd just wrestle for fun."

Micah points to the side of my house where the rosebushes are and gives me a silent smile. As I turn my head, sitting in front of them is a large male lion with a full mane staring right at me. He looks like he is ready to pursue me. I don't know what to do, so I look to Micah for help.

Micah just smiles and says, "Meet Kingsley."

"Kingsley?" Looking back at the lion, I see he is moving toward me. "What do I do?"

Micah points to my Tarzan rope and says, "Better get moving."

I jump up from the picnic table and run to my Tarzan rope. I start pulling myself up, climbing the rope. I can hear the lion panting as he closes in on me. I look over my shoulder to see how close he is, but he has already leaped toward me. I shut my eyes and brace myself for whatever is going to happen.

His roar scares the sh—*crap* out of me. His paws wrap around me, and we both fall to the ground. In that moment, I'm sure I'm going to sustain serious injuries, but we just start wrestling the way Emma and I used to do.

This beast could easily rip me apart, but he just clamps his jaws around my arm and, like Emma, does not bear down. He is certainly bigger and heavier than Emma was, but nonetheless, we just wrestle playfully on the ground.

When we finally stop, he gives me some serious licks on my face. Getting up and looking back to the picnic table, I see Micah almost in tears from laughing so hard. When I walk back and sit down, Kingsley lays down on the grass next to me. Wiping lion saliva from my face and looking at Micah as his laugher subsides, I say, "Real funny. I thought I was going to die . . . again."

Breathing a sigh of relief, I look down at the lion. He licks his lips and paws and lies there peacefully. Petting him, I say, "Well, Kingsley, you scared the . . . ah, well, you scared me good." He just yawns as if to say, "Whatever."

Looking back at Micah, I ask, "Was that your way of answering my question about whether we see our pets in heaven? Or should I ask, more precisely, is such a visualization compatible with love and thus able to be realized?"

"The fright on your face as you were climbing that rope looked pretty real to me." Micah laughs again and then adds, "You have to admit, it was a pretty clever answer to your question, wasn't it? You loved that dog. I still remember when you attached the stuffed rabbit to a fishing line and fed it up over a limb on the maple tree and then to your bathroom window, where you lifted it up as Emma tried to catch it. You drove that dog crazy."

We both laugh at Micah's memory, and he adds, "Any visualization that involves love, yes, it can come to life."

Nodding at Micah's explanation, I ask him, "So I can visualize Tim, Jill, my parents, my sisters, anyone I've loved who . . . well, who has already passed on?"

"You can, and you will, but not just yet. You have more to learn, and you have to extend your awareness considerably. Their level of awareness is well beyond yours at this point, but they know you are here, and they want to meet you too."

"They know I am here?"

"Yes, and it won't be long until you meet them."

"So they all went on a journey like I am going on?"

"Similar, but, as I mentioned before, everyone's journey is different; many of them have advanced considerably."

"What's at the end of their journeys? What's at the end of mine?"

"There is no end, Lou—you will always be on a journey. You will always be learning and growing in God's love, and as you do, so will your joy and understanding grow. I won't always be your guide. You will have many, depending on what path you choose and where you are on that path."

"My journey will take many paths, I take it?"

"There are infinite paths to choose from, my friend, and each may present you with a different guide; some will be assigned, and some you will pick yourself."

"I wouldn't know where to begin as far as choosing a guide, Micah."

"You won't be limited to one, and you can change your guides as you go. Learning is varied and unlimited here. In the earthly realm, you learned many things, some driven by necessity and some driven by interest. That will continue here but will take on many new forms."

"New forms?"

"In the earthly realm, you saw indistinctly, as though you were looking through a cloudy window, but in heaven, you will see clearly, no cloudy windows—crystal clear. In the earthly realm, you knew partially, but in heaven, you will know fully, and in that regard, you are well on your way. You have already begun to learn how visualization can lead to reality, and your awareness is growing by leaps and bounds."

"Really? I trust you on your observation but look forward to progressing."

"Just wait until you meet others and absorb what they know. As you progress, you may desire to learn things you never had time to learn, such as how to play the guitar. I know you love wine. Perhaps you'll want to learn how to make it. You will encounter many guides here to mentor you in whatever you want to pursue. So when I say new forms of learning, I am saying you will grow in ways that you currently do not comprehend."

I nod and try to follow what Micah is sharing with me, and my face lights up. I start to think about the loved ones I left behind. Instead of missing them so deeply, I begin to feel new waves of joy and become excited for them, knowing that they too will be part of this magnificent dynamic life, and I will encounter them when they are.

Looking back at Micah, I ask him, "So there is wine in heaven?"

Nodding, Micah responds, "Of course there is wine in heaven."

CHAPTER 7

God Assignments

> God's plans for you are better than any plans
> you have for yourself. So don't be afraid of
> God's will, even if it's different from yours.
> —Greg Laurie

AGAIN, MY JOY morphs into sadness as I still can't shake the question of "Why me?" I am thinking about so many who are much less fortunate than I am. What about those who die young or, for that matter, die before they are even born?

"I have to ask you, Micah—you said each person's journey is different, and someone who died young would have a shorter journey to . . . well, to heaven. I was thinking about those young people and about the unborn. How do they even start such a journey?"

"Their journey is quite different from yours. Such souls never experienced a cream soda, the feeling of climbing a rope, or a ride on a bike, but they are loved by God just the same. And it's in that love, that perfect love and Spirit of God, that they become full of the same joy you have felt and will continue to feel. Were you thinking about anyone in particular?"

"Yes, first and foremost, I am worried about the loved ones I left behind. I want this joy for them, and I want to be with them."

"You will be with them, Lou, and they will be fine. Remember, God is part of them as he is part of you. On earth, they will enjoy happy times and will also deal with sadness, but the goal is clear: to be here with God and everyone else. God is love, and love gathers. Who else were your thinking about?"

"I was thinking about my niece, Laura. You remember her, don't you?"

"Of course I do. Sweet Laura."

"She was born with so many problems. No one expected her to live one year, yet she lived for eighteen. She brought so many people to God. She couldn't talk and could hardly see, but her parents treated her as if she had no problems at all. They took her everywhere, just like one of their other children, and they loved her equally. She was an angel—at least, that was our understanding of an angel at that time."

Micah smiles. "Why do you say she brought many people to God?"

"Because of the love her parents and her family had for her. They all showed her an exceptional sort of love. When people saw her—still the size of a baby her whole life, even at eighteen—they would take notice and feel bad for her. But when they saw the love her family had for her, how they treated her with dignity and talked to her, even joked with her at times, they felt a true sense of—I don't know—pure love, I guess. And through that love, they were led to faith and to God. That's the best way

I can describe it, anyway. I look at the full life I had and the journey I am now on with you, and I was just wondering about her and many others."

"Children who never learn to speak—like Laura and so many like her, as well as those who never make it to birth—still communicate with God. In fact, Lou, they are totally receptive to him, and remember, they too have a guardian angel who converses with them and guides them."

I look at Micah, happy for Laura and for so many others. "So Laura had an angel?"

"She did. Her name was Dara."

"Dara? Wow. I guess I thought of Laura because I keep thinking about all the things I was blessed with in my life and the journey I am currently on."

"You want her to experience the joy you are experiencing, don't you, Lou?"

"Yes, of course I do. Her life was so restricted and limited."

"It was restricted, yes, but only from *your* perspective was it limited. From God's perspective, her life was far from limited. She understood love, and, as you've said, her love and her family's love brought others into that love—and into God's presence. I want to show you something."

I am thinking how Micah was with me my whole life and how he speaks to God directly, so I just nod in anticipation of what he has to show me.

Micah folds his hands on the picnic table and closes his eyes, appearing as if he is meditating. I notice he is glowing, more so than he normally does.

After about thirty seconds, he opens his eyes and looks at me, and in his normal calm and soothing voice, he says, "I want you to meet someone, Lou," and gestures toward the back of my house.

As I look toward the magnolia tree, I see a woman walking toward us. Her complexion is nothing short of angelic, and she is glowing as she gets closer, her long brown hair bouncing from side to side as she walks. She is wearing a white top and white slacks, both tied with thin white lace rope. Micah gets up and embraces her, whispering into her ear.

She says, ever so softly, "Micah, so good to see you."

As they embrace, they glow even brighter. Another wave of peace flows over me. As they part, Micah looks to me and says, "Well, don't you want to give your niece a hug?"

"My niece?" I look back and forth between the two of them, eyes eventually settling on the angelic woman before me. "Laura?"

With a grin, the woman nods.

I get up and approach her. I believe it's Laura, but I can't help but think about the last time I saw her—she still looked like an infant, even at eighteen. After some hesitation, I say, "Hi, Laura. You are beautiful." Then I think, *Of course she's beautiful. Why wouldn't she be?*

She looks at me. As we embrace, she whispers, "Thank you, Uncle Lou. I remember you always trying to make me smile, and I did a lot. You made me feel happy. Thank you for that."

"I remember, sweetheart. You were so precious and now . . . well, now, you are so beautiful."

As we end our embrace and turn toward the picnic table, still holding hands, we notice that Micah is gone, leaving only Kingsley yawning next to the table. Laura and I walk to the table and sit facing each other. She reaches over, petting Kingsley as if she's known him for a long time. The giant lion leans his head into Laura's touch, loving it, very much like Emma used to do when someone she knew petted her.

"I don't know what to say, Laura," I start off, still in awe. "Are your parents here? Your family? I am all so new to this . . . this new life."

"I know you are, Uncle Lou. Micah asked me to spend some time with you before he continues with your lessons."

"Ah yes, my lessons," I say with a huff of a laugh. "Learning to redefine how I think about imagination and reality. Nothing like the lessons I learned back on earth, right?"

"Well, you never actually left earth, nor did I. We just left the earthly realm. There is a thin layer between heaven and earth."

"So is this heaven?"

"Yes, this is one dimension of heaven. There are multiple dimensions. The earthly realm is another dimension."

"Micah did mention dimensions of heaven briefly to me. I guess I always thought of heaven as a completely different place."

"It is, but it's closer than people think." Laura's brown eyes sparkle in the sunlight, as warm as amber, and I once again have an upsurge of gratitude for everything that has transpired—Magnolia, Micah's guidance, and now Laura's input too. "Heaven isn't some distant, imaginary world or fantasyland. God created heaven and earth, each with its own array of authentic characteristics—some the same, some different, but all connected. You had a full life, Uncle Lou, a good life, and now, you will grow in awareness, and someday you'll reach the ultimate awareness."

"The ultimate awareness? Have you discovered the ultimate awareness, Laura?"

Am I actually asking my niece if she's discovered the ultimate awareness?

Her eyes light up, "Oh yes, Uncle Lou, and you will too. When you do, you will see truth and beauty in everything. And, above all, you will be aware of the presence of God. You've had glimpses of such an awareness in the earthly realm, but here, it will become a constant awareness. It's the difference between dipping your toes into water and immersing yourself fully in it."

I can't help but beam as Laura describes this ultimate awareness to me.

"That's what Micah is teaching you. There is a process of letting go before you can fully invite the divine into your awareness. Relax and trust his guidance. He's already introduced you to the power of visualization, of which I am one result." And after a slight pause, she adds, "Like that brownie."

I snicker, shaking my head. "How did you know about the brownie?"

Laura continues to laugh and then says, "We communicate a little differently here, Uncle Lou."

"Well, yeah, I think I'm going to find out a lot of things are different here, Laura."

As our laughter subsides, Laura tells me, "Communication here is a lot like the roots of a tree. Did you know that many trees communicate with each other through their root systems? They can warn each other about drought or disease, insect infestations, and more—all through communication that occurs through their roots."

"I . . . had no idea," I say truthfully.

"They are always connected, always aware of one another," she says. "Here, we're all connected, just like the roots of every tree in a forest. We can tap into one another at will, effortlessly, and almost immediately."

My jaw drops, and I shake my head. "And I'll be able to do this too?"

"Of course," she says. "You'll be able to check in on all of us, on matters big, small, and everything in between. For me, that meant checking in to see my Uncle Lou eating a brownie he visualized from his childhood at the Magnolia Bakery." She winks.

"I guess it's like the internet."

"The internet? Oh, the computer network thing?" She laughs, tossing a curtain of silky brown hair over her shoulder. "Hardly that limited, but I guess from your perspective, yes, that is a primitive example."

"Primitive." I raise my brows, laughing. "Well, I guess from everything I've seen so far, you're probably right—very primitive." After a pause, I ask, "Laura, it's just so amazing being on this journey and especially seeing and talking with you. What do you do here?"

"What do I do? You mean like things you did in the earthly realm?"

"I guess, yes—I mean, when you're not helping your Uncle Lou, guiding him on such an amazing journey."

"Well, there is no limit to what I can do. As your awareness grows and you begin to feel God's presence, you will be able to communicate with him, and he will direct you down many paths—paths that are much more important than learning how to play the guitar. And when you pursue something on such a path, your joy will be overflowing."

"Has God helped you pursue such things?"

"Oh my, Uncle Lou, yes, so many things. As Micah told you, we all are assigned a guardian angel when we are first conceived. For those who die before they're born and other children who die young, I help their guardian angels with the transition. Many times, that simply involves holding them and loving them during those initial stages. I love it! It's like our hearts melt into each other. When you and I embraced, you must have felt that energy flowing between us."

"I did. It felt amazing. I didn't know what was happening. We started to glow as we embraced."

"Unbelievable, right?" Laura's eyes soften as she says, "You will feel that exchange with everyone you meet here. With young children, I know their parents worry that they are safe, so I work with the child's guardian angel and the parents' guardian angels and others to try and comfort their souls."

Suddenly, another wave of realization strikes, powerful enough to knock me off balance. Tears burn along my eyelids just thinking about how devastated and afraid a new soul might be after being introduced to life, only to have it stolen away.

The reality that there are angels available to support those souls is a kindness that I always hoped existed. To know that it actually does, that all this is by God's design, is a new level of optimism and joy I've never felt before.

Laura doesn't stop speaking, though she does notice my rising emotions and sets a soft hand on my forearm. "As you grow in awareness, Uncle Lou, you will realize everyone is connected here. It's like we are all related—all family. Remember when you traveled for work or waited in a doctor's office or just went to the mall? Remember feeling alone because you didn't know anyone? They were all strangers to you."

I pause, reflecting on those moments of sitting in a stream of traffic, angry over getting home late. "Sometimes it felt like I was the only person who existed in the world, outside my family. Everybody else—those strangers—all felt like background noise. It's hard trusting strangers, the public. It wasn't like that when I was a child growing up, but in my later years, I really felt that division."

"That division is part of the human experience," Laura says vaguely, mouth falling into something of a frown. "As were my physical and mental limitations while I was alive. I watched as the rest of the world embraced life in a way I never could, and that felt isolating—but that part of life is one of the most important parts."

"Isolation?"

"Individuation," she clarifies. "The solitude. The loneliness, even. It all serves as a lesson we can't quite learn in heaven, where we're all connected."

"Is that why I felt such a rush of relief when I was in a room full of strangers and I spotted somebody familiar?" I ask. "It was like a light in the darkness. When I saw a friend or relative in that setting, the loneliness evaporated, and we were drawn together like a pair of magnets."

"Remember during your third visit to Magnolia, when you were on the backstop, enjoying the feeling of being pain free and having all that energy again?"

"Wow, you do get around Laura." I laugh, reflecting back on that moment. "Yes, sitting up on that backstop without being in pain anymore and without constantly coughing—that was the best."

"Yet you felt a wave of distress. Something was . . . missing."

"Yes, I felt lonely." I shrug, realizing how funny it is that I was experiencing a taste of real-life heaven—without pain or suffering—and yet it felt empty without my family.

Heaven felt empty without my family.

Laura sits back, seemingly observing the cogs turning in my mind.

I clear my throat. "I was missing my family. I was missing the feeling of knowing I was always going to be with them at suppertime."

"When you were young, back in Magnolia, the love of your family was always with you wherever you were—whether on foot or on that black Schwinn bike of yours. Even when you were doing things you knew you shouldn't have been doing, like running through the sewer pipes." As Laura says that, we both break into laughter.

"You're right. I never felt lonely. I always had my family and friends around. Sisters, cousins, so many friends—even when I really was alone, I never felt lonely, if that makes any sense."

"It makes perfect sense, Uncle Lou, and I am here to tell you that you will never feel lonely again. You will have alone time, but just like on that backstop when you were a kid, you will feel a presence around you. The presence of not just your family and friends but of all souls—of all people. That comfort will come from everyone. They will all be your friends and relatives. No one will be a stranger to you again."

"Are you saying I will know everyone?"

"The same way information is shared, love is also shared. You see, Uncle Lou, you are on a journey, and you will grow in love, joy, peace, patience, kindness, generosity, faithfulness, gentleness, understanding, and so much more. Everyone here is on that journey, and although our journeys are a little different, they lead to the same destination of acquiring those traits. So when we encounter each other, we encounter someone very much like us—someone growing in understanding."

I allow this information to settle into place, pondering the experience of now being able to identify and relate with perfect strangers. It's a powerful feeling, and one I am very excited to acquaint myself with—but it doesn't change the fact that right now, fresh into all this, I'm still focused on reconnecting with my family. With this thought, I begin to visualize Timmy. I am seeing his playful smile and his bushy brown hair. And with that thought, I visualize hugging him and feeling him alive in my arms.

"Laura." I swallow back tears. "I would love to see my Timmy again."

She continues to smile and then gestures toward the rosebushes.

As I turn my head, I see a boy standing next to the orange roses that go up the side of the white garage. I look closer and see it is my son. He is just as I visualized him: bushy brown hair, blue jeans, and a faded yellow T-shirt. Losing all form of control, I jump from the picnic table, yelling "Timmy!" as I run toward him, and he runs toward me.

We meet and embrace each other tightly.

"Timmy, I've missed you so much!" As I hold him, I feel a flow of energy between us that is unlike anything I've ever felt before. We fall to the grass, and I hold him, kissing his forehead. "Oh, Timmy! Are you real? Is it you? I've missed you so much!"

"I am real, Dad, and I missed you too. I am so glad to see you. I knew you would be here. I can't even tell you how much you will love it."

We get up, still embracing, and walk back to the picnic table. "I am so sorry you drowned." Tears flow uncontrollably. "I never wanted to let you go on that camping trip, but all your friends were going. Almost every day after that, I wished so much that I could go back in time and keep you from going and keep you home with us that weekend."

Timmy looks back up at me, and we embrace harder. "It's all right, Dad. We are together now, and we can be together anytime we want to. I met my guardian angel, Nathaniel, that day. He was amazing. I was so worried about you and Mom being so upset, but he assured me we would all be together again, and we are."

"I am still trying to believe it, Tim."

"Just let it happen, Dad. Follow Micah's lead, and you will come to an unbelievable understanding and awareness."

"Have you seen your mother?"

"Yes, and you will too. Micah will show you through it all. There is so much love here, Dad, and so much beauty. And the most magnificent part of all this is that you will meet God."

As Timmy says this, I have no idea what expression forms on my face, but I feel as though I am in a stream of ever-flowing love.

Timmy and Laura and I sit at the picnic table for what seems like hours. Holding their hands and gazing at both of them, I tell them, "I am so happy."

Timmy and Laura get up from the picnic table at the same time, and immediately I feel my heart sink. *Where are they going?*

Laura's brown eyes soften. "We will talk again, Uncle Lou. Remember, there is only love here. The kingdom of God is the way of ordering things born of love—love for God and love for neighbor. Remember the lesson of the backstop: when you were young and gazing up at the clouds, you felt surrounded by the love of friends and family. Loneliness never entered your thoughts. You were overflowing with joy. And now, you will again overflow with joy but even more so."

"But you haven't even left yet, and I feel like I miss you," I confess.

"No need, Dad," Tim says, smirking. "We'll see you at the party soon."

Before I can ask what party he's talking about, they turn and disappear behind the wall of foliage bordering my property in Magnolia.

I look down at Kingsley, who is resting peacefully. "What party, Kingsley?" Kingsley just ignores me, so I decide to spring up and get into a wrestling stance in front of him. The lion immediately gets into an attack stance as if to say, "Oh really? You want some of this?"

"No, no, no. Relax, Kingsley. Just testing you."

CHAPTER 8

There Is Only Now

> Life gives you plenty of time to do
> whatever you want to do if you
> stay in the present moment.
> —Deepak Chopra

SOON ENOUGH, I see Micah walking back to me. He sits across from me at the picnic table and asks me, "How was your visit with Tim and Laura?"

I shake my head, still in a state of disbelief. "What can I say, Micah? It was amazing—but amazing doesn't come close to describing them or this journey or *any* of this. I can't tell you how I have longed to see my son again, to know he's safe and happy. I saw that happiness on his face, and I felt his joy when we embraced. I want to tell God directly how . . . how thankful I am. There are no words, Micah."

"He already knows how thankful you are, but you will get your chance to tell him directly. Trust me on that. Now, what do you say we change the scenery?"

"Leave my backyard? Why not?"

"Where would you like to go?"

"Where, indeed?" I look around the yard and then back to Micah. "I don't know . . . . How about Italy?"

"When you say Italy, what are you imagining?"

I giggle a bit, realizing Micah is taking me seriously. "I am visualizing sitting at an outdoor café, sipping on a cappuccino."

Micah reaches for my hands and tells me to relax and visualize the café in Italy.

Smiling and closing my eyes as we hold hands, I clear my mind and start to visualize a quiet scene in a piazza outside a corner café with small tables and, of course, a fountain nearby. People at a few of the tables are speaking Italian while others walk by, simply enjoying the nice day.

I breathe deeply, visualizing every detail of the scene.

Micah says calmly, "Open your eyes, Lou."

Before I even open my eyes, I start to hear chatter in both Italian and English around me. I open my eyes, and there we are, sitting at a small round table still holding hands. Looking around, I see a larger fountain in the center of a piazza, a row of shops, and waiters serving tables around me. In the distance, I see part of the Colosseum and then, looking at Micah, I smile and say, "Yep, this sure looks like Rome."

"It is Rome, Lou. You brought it to life."

"Just like I brought that brownie to life?"

"Yes, but I would say on a much grander scale, wouldn't you?"

"I would say so, yes."

I am still looking around and taking the sights and sounds in when a waiter comes over and says, "*Buongiorno* Luigi *e* Micah. *Cosa posso portarti?*"

Micah nods, smiling. Then, looking to me, he says, "Roberto says hi and wants to know what he can get for us."

At that, Roberto grabs my hand, and as he does, I feel a warm energy, almost like an electrical current, flowing between us. It is pleasant and joyful, sort of like the feeling when Tim and I embraced. Roberto smiles, for he apparently feels it as well.

"Welcome, Lou. How about that cappuccino?" he suggests. "And let me bring you a surprise with it, if I may."

I grin up at Roberto, nodding. "Sure. And thank you, Roberto. It's great meeting you and being here."

As Roberto walks off, I look at Micah. "Are we really in Italy? In Rome?"

"Indeed we are, my friend."

"So do the same rules apply for visualizing places as for visualizing people?

"For the most part, yes. A few things are different, but love is the key."

"Can I visualize an earlier time? Like, can I go back in time?"

Micah gives me a look that suggests he knew this question was coming.

The truth is, it's a question I've entertained most of my life, and I am sure he knew it was coming.

"No," he says finally. "No time travel in heaven. You can visualize places that no longer exist and make them come to life, but you can't recreate life events that have already occurred. In a way, I did that in Magnolia. The oak tree in your yard fell down years ago, but I was able to recreate it the way you remembered. But I could not recreate the time you fell out of it. That life event already happened. The people we encounter in heaven are current—not past. You encountered your mom as she is today, here in heaven, as you did with Miss Pettengill and with Tim and Laura. You have memories of them in the past, but they exist here and now in this dimension of heaven."

I nod as Micah tries to explain heaven and time to me.

He goes on to add, "Heaven is a place of eternal peace and joy, so there's no need for us to go back in time or forward into the future. We will have all eternity to enjoy the presence of God and of each other without worrying about what has been or what will be."

With somewhat of a bewildered look, I attempt to react to Micah's explanation. "So there is only . . . *now*?"

"Yes, Lou. Time is a dimension of the physical universe. Material things need time to exist. Heaven is outside the physical universe, as are you. We are in the spiritual realm; there is no time here. You can think of this as an eternity, or you can view it as an instant of pure bliss that has no ending. So, Lou, eternity takes over now to introduce you to the timelessness of truth, peace, and love."

At that, Roberto brings us our cappuccinos, along with a special lemon pastry of some type. He says, "I made you a special limoncello tartufo." It looks like a ball of vanilla gelato with a lemon-flavored white chocolate shell. Roberto smiles. "Enjoy, Luigi."

As I sip my cappuccino and take a spoonful of the limoncello tartufo, I look at Micah and say, "This is indeed pure bliss, and I thank God it has no ending." I look at the people sitting around me. Some are alone, some are with someone else, and there is one table that looks like a bunch of friends. Some smile at me and wave as if they know me. I look back at Micah.

"They do know you, Lou—and you know them."

"I really don't."

"But you do. You know everyone, and everyone knows you. Remember Laura's discussion. There are no more strangers. There is only love. Look at that couple." Micah points to a man and woman sitting near us. "Clear your mind and concentrate on them for a moment."

Sipping my cappuccino, I look at them and notice that they appear very vibrant—as does everyone here, for that matter. Their faces have that glow as well. I close my eyes, and as I do, my mind becomes infused with something. I don't know how to describe it. It's like the essence of who they are. Waves of joy flow over me, and I feel myself becoming very close to them, almost to the point where I feel I should go and hug them and ask them what they are doing here in this café, the same way I would if I were to run into relatives unexpectedly here in Italy.

Opening my eyes, I stand and look at them. When we make eye contact, we smile, walk toward each other, and embrace. "Santino and Kim!" They aren't relatives, but I know them just as well—and they know me. It dawns on me that Roberto probably knows me this well too.

They smile. "So nice to see you, Lou."

After chatting a bit, I walk back to Micah. "It's interesting, what Laura told me—there are no strangers here."

"Yes, Lou, and the love you feel is a process—a process because it keeps growing as you grow in knowledge and awareness."

"I remember hearing there were different kinds of love. Is this a certain type of love?"

"People in the earthly realm tend to categorize and label everything—but no, there are no kinds of love here. Love is love. It takes many shapes. It can come into the world as compassion, kindness, service, and sacrifice. No matter how you express your loving impulses, they have their origin in God. Each time you are inspired to reach out to help another, you are bringing love into the world. When your heart is opened and you are moved to tears, you are responding in love. When you place another's wants or needs before your own, you are acting from love. God is love and from now on, you will express and act out what you know of love. You will do this at each stage of your growth here, and from my view, you are progressing well."

"And the idea of no strangers in heaven . . . . I just felt that with Santino and Kim."

"It's human nature—another one of those things that society and culture have clouded back in the earthly realm. God created this need for togetherness in all his creations. It's limitless, as is love. Everyone is eager to be recognized, waiting to develop, and yearning to grow."

"What gets in our way, Micah?"

"Many things, Lou. For one, the fear of change is a deterrent to love, and that is unfortunate because, as you know, change is an inevitable part of life. Attitudes, feelings, desires, and even who we are as people—that all changes. There is no stopping that change—only accepting it and adapting to it."

I take a sip of my cappuccino, the flavor smooth and rich. I can't believe I'm sitting here in Italy right now, in the heart of Rome, speaking to my guardian angel after reuniting with my late son and niece.

It's incredible. It's so incredible.

I'm itching to see my wife again, after all these years.

"There is a Hindu tale," Micah goes on, "about a man in a small boat rowing up a fast-flowing river against the current. After a great battle, he finally discovers the effort is futile, so he raises his oars and begins to sing. The moment teaches him a new way of life; only when he goes with the changing river is he truly free. So yes, Lou, fear gets in the way, but love will ultimately not be deterred. It flows like that river—always itself, yet ever changing, recognizing no obstacles. And now? It's your time to sing."

"When I was hugging Santino and Kim, I did feel like that was me singing but not actually singing."

"Well, what you will find—and you would have found it in the earthly realm, to some extent—is that all people are interconnected, and each person who comes closer to themselves in any way becomes closer to others. So now, think of it as a dual journey. It's what love is all about and what Laura introduced you to back in Magnolia. The best definition of love I've ever heard is from Antoine de Saint-Exupéry, a French writer, poet, journalist, and pioneering aviator. He defined love as 'the process of my leading you back to yourself.' We all have the ability to guide one another to love. It's just a matter of using that ability, Lou."

I look at Santino and Kim and feel such a closeness with them. "Is it like this with everyone?"

Micah glows a little brighter as he smiles and says, "Yes, and eventually it will come naturally to you. Want to try again?"

I nod, though I am hesitant. Naturally, Micah senses my hesitance and notices that something is troubling me. Before he can ask, I say, "Does it matter who I pick? I mean, there are no strangers here, right?"

"No, it doesn't matter," he says. "But that's not what is troubling you, is it, Lou?"

Already I feel tears accumulating in my eyes. "I can't help but notice that some of these people are alone, some are with friends, and others seem to be couples . . . loving couples."

Micah holds my hand again and asks me, "You mean a couple like you and Jill?"

"Well, yes—a place like this makes me miss her. Believe me, I understand I have a lot to learn, and I am just starting my journey, but as I look around at these people, it just instills a desire in me to be sitting here with her." I shrug, looking Micah in the eyes. "I was able to see my son and my niece. Why not my wife?"

"Of course, you will sit here with Jill. I just wanted to expose you to the love principles that Laura introduced you to, particularly as they pertain to understanding how we are all connected in love here—from you and me to Santino and Kim to everyone in this piazza and certainly to Jill."

"Thank you, Micah. It's not that I doubted your guidance or anything; I just wanted to let you know how much she has been on my mind. I know I will eventually see her, and I guess she has been on mind even more now that I saw Tim and Laura."

"I understand. Jill passed just over thirty years now, and you were married, what? Forty-five years?"

"Yes. Hard to believe all that time went by." As I think about Jill and all the things we did together, I look around the café, seeing all the couples smiling and chatting as they enjoy a coffee. "Are people married here, Micah?"

"The joining of a couple through marriage is the second most important relationship in one's life. The most important is your relationship with God, of course. But, here in heaven, marriages just aren't needed as they are in the earthly realm. That is not to say you can't continue a relationship with Jill. Many couples continue their relationships. They just change. *You've* changed, my friend. You are more like me now. We are spiritual beings. There is no marriage in heaven simply because there is no need for it. Remember, it was God who established marriage, and he did so to fill certain needs. It helps for countless reasons to love somebody so much that you're willing to partner with them for life. That is a taste of the love you'll feel for everybody here."

I take a sip of my cappuccino. "That's hard to wrap my mind around, Micah."

"It is a process," he admits, nodding. "Just try to remember that here in heaven, as you've just begun to see, there is no loneliness, nor is there any need for helpers. You are surrounded by believers and angels, and all your needs will be met, including the need for companionship. Think back to when you hugged Santino and Kim. Do you remember that feeling?"

"It was like our—I don't know—our *essences* flowed back and forth to one another. I felt like I'd always known them, and now I know them better than anyone . . ." I pause for a moment. "Better than anyone."

"The knowing of each other brings joy—an integral act of love. The bond and interconnection you have to the believers here is endless, not just with those you knew in the earthly realm but with all the believers across time who once lived." He smiles warmly and touches my arm. "And that certainly includes Jill."

As Micah sees a more relaxed expression return to my face, he adds, "And when you meet Jill and embrace her, you will perceive the woman she has become—how her spirit has grown and continues to grow."

This shifts my mood in a better direction. I've missed that woman so much, and to think that I've got the blessing of meeting and falling in love with her twice—two different iterations of her, in life and after it—is one of the greatest gifts I could ever conceive of.

"That is exciting," I say, even though *exciting* doesn't even cover it. "So we can be together as much as we want, just like everyone here? And with that comes an ever-growing love for each other?"

Micah nods with a look of delight. "And for God."

Smiling at him, I say, "I guess I haven't quite mastered this flip-flopping from physical to spiritual and all that's involved with it."

"You are doing magnificently, Lou. Eventually, your mind will be more connected to spiritual things than to physical things, but the spiritual can still manifest into physical. A hug is a hug, but the transfer, in addition to the physical touch, is a *spiritual* exchange allowing love to flow between people. And with that, love flows with understanding and awareness."

Holding up my last spoonful of limoncello tartufo, I ask Micah, "This is real, though, right?"

"It's real," he says, eyeing the tartufo. "And thanks for sharing, by the way."

"Come on, angels don't eat tartufo."

Micah smiles. "But saints do, huh?"

CHAPTER 9

I Feel You

> No one has ever seen God; but if we love one another, God lives in us and his love is made complete in us.
>
> —1 John 4:12

I RAISE MY brows at Micah, chewing the last bite of my limoncello tartufo. The lemon-flavored white chocolate has blended nicely with the melted vanilla gelato. "Don't even begin to call me a saint, Micah."

"Why?" he asks innocently. "What is your understanding of a saint?"

"Oh, I don't know," I say, waving my spoon around. "Someone who dedicated their whole life to God? Certainly not me. I already told you—I don't think I deserve this."

"Well, my friend, all souls in heaven are saints. In the earthly realm, many religions established criteria for who may be referred to as a saint, based on how they lived their life, but that was their best guess on who would go to heaven and who would not. There is nothing wrong with that, except their effort to predict who was worthy of heaven and who wasn't. God is the only one who can make that judgment. If you are here, you are a spirit in heaven—*saint* is just another name for you, just like the word *angel* is another word for me."

"Eventually, this will all sink in, won't it?"

"Oh, it will sink in all right, Lou. In fact, you are about to set forth on a small journey all on your own. The journey will move you much closer to a point where things will start to click."

"On my own?" I balk. "With my current awareness of heaven and myself? Are you sure I'm ready for that?"

"Of course not, Lou," Micah replies, laughing. I stare, jaw agape and even slightly afraid, despite being in literal heaven. "But in your lifetime, how many situations were you ready for?"

"I was ready for some of them, at least, Micah."

"You will be fine, and when you are ready to come back to me, all you have to do is visualize yourself sitting with me at the picnic table in your yard in Magnolia. Simple enough, right?"

"I don't know where to begin." Even though I am in heaven, my emotions still fluctuate between extreme joy and uneasiness. I look to Micah for guidance. "What sort of journey is this? And how do I start?"

"Let's talk about what you already know, my friend. You are safe. You are loved. You are never alone." He waves an arm, gesturing to the people perusing Italy around us, all of whom I somehow know and am connected to. "And you are right where God wants you to be. You've already experienced the power of visualization for meeting people and going places. You've seen how an embrace here allows another's joy, peace, and a good deal of wisdom to pass between the two of you. Granted, in the beginning, more will flow into you than out of you," he notes, and I furrow my brow. "But eventually, it will be an even, two-way flow. When you meet people here, you do more than say hi and go your own way. You really encounter them as if you already know them. That knowing will change every time because the next time you meet, you will both have grown and expanded in various ways."

I nod apprehensively. "I hear you, Mr. Guardian, and I thank you for . . . well, for this journey. Whatever it will look like."

"No, Lou, I thank you for this," Micah says, ignoring my sarcasm. "This is just the beginning for you, and you are on this path because of the good life you lived. It is a privilege to be able to watch you grow spiritually now. I do have a starting point for you, however. And then we will meet back in Magnolia whenever you are ready. Don't forget, there's no time here, Lou. Travel. Meet people. Grow. Learn. Be. Love."

"I will, Micah. I will. You said you have a starting point for me?"

"Yes. There is someone I want you to meet before you start your journey."

"Another angel?"

"Another saint." He gestures to a small table in the café. I turn and look; a woman is sitting there and smiling at me. She definitely looks familiar. As I focus, I see it's Jill.

I know Micah claims time doesn't exist here, but it sure does feel like time stops.

Knowing that it is, I ask anyway, voice shaking. "Can that be Jill?"

When Micah doesn't reply, I look back at him, only to realize he's gone. I'm not sure I have a beating heart anymore, but something's beating throughout my body as I get up and walk to her. "Oh my God. Jill?"

I move faster as she stands and walks toward me. I see her face and her amazing smile—a smile I have never forgotten. I reach for her, and we embrace. "Oh, Jill, is this really you?" I squeeze her, taking in her scent and essence.

"It's me, Lou. I've looked forward to you being here. It's amazing, isn't it?"

I release my tight hold on her and gaze into her eyes. "Amazing? It's just unbelievable." I hold her tight again, and it's like when I embraced Santino and Kim. There is a flow of warmth pouring in to me—a beautiful flow of love, joy, and peace. But now, with Jill, there's even more than that. I feel like we're meeting all over again. So much knowledge is exchanged in our embrace.

I sense music as well. Don't ask me how, but some form of rhythm and harmony fills my senses as we embrace. Yes, this is my wife from the earthly realm, but there is so much more.

I see what Micah was trying to tell me. Jill's spirit has continued to grow in so many ways after she entered the beyond. As we loosen our embrace, we continue to gaze at each other, my eyes drinking her in like water after too much time in the sun—those hazel eyes, fanned with dark lashes, and a face as young as the day I'd met her. But what's most striking and beautiful is the wisdom she embodies, which she had only a pinprick of while alive. I hope to someday reach her level. I hope she'll help me reach her level.

"Jill," I say, voice a rasp. "Look at you."

We embrace again, her head tucked under my chin. Voice buried in my chest, she says, "It's me, Lou." With that, she pulls away, giving me a once-over. "And look at you."

Tears pour from my eyes. "Have you seen Tim?"

"Yes, of course I have. Isn't he amazing?"

"Oh, Jill, yes, he is, and so are you, and so is all this. Can you believe it?"

"I believe it, all right. We are here, Lou, hugging in heaven!"

Eventually, we sit down, still holding hands. At some point, Roberto returns to the table and offers us both fresh coffee. I receive a cappuccino without even asking, and he brings over Jill's favorite: a shot of espresso.

He really does know us like family. Everybody here does.

"When I hugged you," I tell Jill, still in awe, "so much of your spirit flowed into me that I even sensed music, like a piano or something."

Jill chuckles and sips her espresso. "When people embrace here, it's quite different from embracing in the physical world. Here, it's a spiritual exchange. You'll feel a flow of energy and awareness and consciousness coming into you—not everything because, in some cases, there is just so much. Some spirits have grown more than others. It's like you receive what you need—what you're ready for—at the time you embrace."

"That is phenomenal," I say, still staring at her like she's a celebrity and I'm some rabid fan, starstruck to the point of paralysis. *This is my wife. This was my partner in life, and we had kids together. And now, we're here.*

"It's like that movie we watched years ago," Jill says. "*Avatar*. When a creature connects their tendrils with those of another being, it enables mental communication between the two entities and the sharing of information, including memories, emotions, and sensory input. You will experience this more and more. And yes, I've taken up the piano," she adds, almost preening. "And I love it."

"Wait, don't tell me—Ludwig van Beethoven is your teacher."

Jill looks puzzled for a split second, then starts laughing hysterically. "No, I'm afraid not. Just a woman I met who has been so patient with me and has taken me so far. I never had any interest in learning a musical instrument in the earthly realm. But here, everyone understands each other and loves each other and wants to help each other. We all look at one another from the perspective of 'What can I do to help this spirit?' You can learn anything you want."

"The thought of not having such an unlimited and ever-growing life is truly hell. Will I be able to thank God directly, Jill? Did you?"

With that question, Jill glows brighter, and with the warmest smile I have ever seen from her, she says, "Yes I did and so will you."

Jill's answer stuns me for a while but after recovering, we begin reminiscing about how we met, our children, our jobs, our homes, our trips, one life segment after the next—all the things you would expect a couple married for forty-five years would want to talk about. Jill looks deeply into my eyes, squeezes my hands, and says, "I've missed you, Lou, and I must tell you how much I regret blaming you for what happened to Timmy."

"It was such a hard time. Our lives changed for sure, Jill, but thank God for your faith. It got us through."

"It helped, but we were never the same. I blamed you for letting him go on that trip. After being here and with the help of so many, I realize that, and I tried to communicate it to you in so many ways."

"We were only human, Jill. So many couples break up after they go through something like that. But you're right; we were never the same. We never achieved the happiness we once had, and I know it affected Mikey immensely. But surely the joy of being here has washed those feeling away."

"Washed them away? Yes, I can see Micah has had an effect on you already. That's a great way to phrase that. Yes, there's so much joy here, Lou, and it does wash away any lingering regrets and sadness. I know the years following Timmy's death affected Mike. I worked with my guardian angel, Seraphina, to try and comfort him through my prayers."

"I think they worked. He turned out all right. He met a good woman and had two amazing girls, who loved you very much, as you know."

"They are so precious. I hated not being there for them, but Seraphina assured me they were in good hands."

"They are amazing teenagers now and involved in so many things. Mike and Emily are great parents. As for their relationship to God, I know Timmy's accident made God seem unreal to Mike, and that lack of faith spread through his family, but I think their faith will grow. I already saw signs of that, and Mike promised me he would at least keep the door open."

For a few moments, we just gaze at each other. I ask, "You know what I missed most about you? I missed our quiet times on Saturday morning, enjoying our coffee together."

"Yes, They were precious moments. The trips and vacations and the houses and jobs were . . . well, they were big things, but yes, those small things like enjoying our coffee together were the best."

But as we talk, it becomes very clear to me that things are different. For one thing, we are both in heaven. You would expect my memories of the earthly realm to be much fresher than Jill's since she died over thirty years ago, but that's not the case. Her memory puts mine to shame. In fact, I have never known Jill to be so crystal clear and so sharp when recalling events. I also sense an awareness that emanates from her. This must be what Micah described. Eventually, our attention moves to the present—the eternal now that we are both living.

"We were married for so many years, Jill," I say, reflecting now on the harder times we had endured together. It wasn't always easy. "What if we had divorced and remarried other people? Would we still meet like this?"

Jill giggles. "Still the analytical Lou I've always known, I see. There is no marriage or divorce here. Everyone knows everyone, and love is the binding force. You and I have a history in the earthly realm—a good history, a loving history—but here, we are just loving spirits. We can be together whenever you want to be together, but we are still being perfected, and that perfection is guided by love. Remember, we love everybody equally in this heavenly realm. If we had divorced and remarried, I would love your new wife as much as I love you, and I would know her just as well too."

I take a deep breath and look at Jill as if I am in a trance. "I know I have so much to learn. The biggest thing for me to understand is this flip-flopping between the spiritual and physical."

"Ah, yeah, well . . ." She touches my hand, squeezing it. "We may be in the spiritual realm, and we may be spirits, but we're still holding each other's hand, are we not?"

Looking at our hands and grasping Jill's tighter, I say, "We absolutely are, and that limoncello tartufo I just ate? That was mouthwatering."

Jill giggles. "As was that brownie from the Magnolia Bakery."

"Oh wow, there are no secrets here," I say, laughing and blushing a little.

"Not really," she says. "Someday, you'll take comfort in this level of connection."

"That's going to be an adjustment for me."

"It's less about not having any privacy and more about always being understood," she explains, and I allow that to settle in. Immediately, I'm drenched in a feeling of relief—the idea of never again being judged by others is truly heaven.

"Well, when you put it that way, I can get behind it."

"I can't take credit for that particular breakdown," she says, smiling. "My guardian, Seraphina, explained it to me that way when I was in your shoes, and it made all the difference for me as well. She has done so well, guiding me through all this."

"What about other physical things?" I ask. "I mean, well . . . you know what I mean, Jill."

Jill smiles. "Sex?"

"Well, yes. I mean, that's physical like the tartufo, in a way, isn't it?"

Jill looks warmly at me. "It's physical, but it's not like a tartufo. One of the many things you will learn about the spiritual realm, Lou, is the absolute wonder of creation. Back in the earthly realm, we saw glimpses of it. Remember our discussions about how the body was a miracle and how the earth and its systems were so perfect?"

"Yes, I remember talking about a tree in the winter and how its branches were like the nerves or blood vessels in our body or the bronchi in our lungs. We knew there was something to it; we sensed the magnificence and brilliance of it all, but it was beyond our comprehension."

"Exactly. But now, it's no longer beyond our comprehension, Lou. As you grow in spirit and awareness, your thoughts and desires will change. A tartufo will always taste good to you, as will a good bottle of wine, and they are both available here, but as far as your sex drive is concerned, it changes considerably. There is no longing for sex anymore. You will find that there are far greater pleasures. I will look forward to seeing you discovering that, and you will, but for now, just know that the appetites and desires we had in the earthly realm give way to higher and infinitely more gratifying delights in this spiritual realm."

"You are helping me a lot, Jill." I peer around the café at the people walking by, a plethora of faces, appearances—ages. "How is it that some people seem younger and some seem older, but there are no small children or old people?"

"You've met Laura, right?"

"Yes."

"As you know, she died at eighteen, but on earth, she looked more like an infant. After she passed and her guardian angel guided her into the spiritual realm, she realized, like you did, that she was blessed with a glorious body—a body with no earthly defects—and that's how you saw her."

"Wow," I say, stunned by it all. "That's wonderful." I pause for a moment. "The many children who died young or even before birth—does God also give them glorified bodies?"

"Yes. Regardless of our earthly body, God transforms our spiritual body so it will be like his glorious body."

"No more lower back pain?"

"No, silly. How else were you able to climb that Tarzan rope?"

Jill giggles, and I study her, still amazed by the fact she is somebody I loved and lost thirty years ago. Her appearance is youthful, but not so young that I wouldn't recognize her.

I look down at my body—my arms, without gray hair and age spots. "I suppose older people like me end up in a younger, energetic body," I say. "I didn't even mean to visualize this, but I already have."

Jill nods slowly, smile broadening. "You were able to ride your bike and climb the backstop at the schoolyard and climb your Tarzan rope—except not fast enough to get away from Kingsley," she adds with a laugh.

"No, he was quicker than I estimated."

"He's a lion," she rebuts, cocking a brow. "What did you expect?"

We share a laugh at that and comfortably sip our coffees. The sun begins to set in the distance, nesting over the horizon. "So what do I look like right now?" I ask her, all of a sudden feeling vulnerable. I hold out my younger arms, inhaling deeply through my young and clear lungs. "How old do I look?"

"Definitely a question from the earthly realm since there is really no concept of age here, but it's a fair question, so I would say you look about thirty years old."

We sit in silence for a while, enjoying the peace of the moment. I'm still trying and failing to wrap my head around the fact that this is going to be what it's like for me for the rest of eternity. *Forever.* I've got a long journey ahead of me, but it is still a little scary to think about eternity and filling all that time. Won't I get sick of myself? Won't I grow bored? Won't I, at some point, learn everything there is to learn?

For now, I push the thought away, labeling it as something I'll pester Micah about later. "So," I ask, "how do you think I should start my journey? Micah wants me to go on my own and then meet back up with him. Supposedly, I can go anywhere and talk to anyone. That covers a lot of ground. Where do I even begin?"

"Well, I personally started with my dad," she says, smirking. "No surprise there, right? You know how close we were—and now, we still are. But Seraphina suggested I take time and pray about who I should meet, so I did."

"So praying is still part of life here in heaven?"

"Of course, Lou; we still have free will. We just can't get hurt anymore, and because of our genuine love for everybody else, we can't hurt anybody either. But we can always use God's guidance. Remember, this is just the beginning of a new journey, and it all begins with trust."

"Trust? Trust myself? Trust Micah? Trust God?"

"Yes, to all three. When you were in the earthly realm, had you known you had a guardian angel, would you have trusted him?"

"I definitely would have trusted Micah."

"Especially when you found out that God speaks through him, right?"

"Absolutely. I wish I had known that. Micah told me we can contact those still living through prayer."

"We do our best, but there are so many obstacles to our prayers back in the earthly realm, we don't often get through. I am sure Micah will tell you more about that. The good news, Lou, is that God is still guiding you—but now, you are aware of it. So why don't you ask him for help? You should construct a small prayer, asking him to guide you on this journey. Then trust him and set out on your way."

"A small prayer," I say, mulling it over. "Can you help me?"

"Of course I can." Jill takes my hands and smiles at me tenderly as she devises a prayer. "'Praise to you, Lord, our God, maker of heaven and earth and all things, who brings life to our body and spirit and imparts peace and joy on us. Guide Lou on his journey to know you through your children.' How's that?"

"That sounded good. So now what do I do? Wait until someone comes to my mind and then do the visualization thing?"

"You could. Think about that prayer or one like it, and just relax. Order another cappuccino and take in the sights until you feel inspired. I will leave you now but will see you again, Lou." Jill gets up to hug me, and again, I feel a flow of energy coming from her as we embrace and say goodbye for now. She adds, "See you at the party."

"What party?"

She just smiles and walks away.

CHAPTER 10

A Nobody from New Jersey

> But the wisdom from above is first
> of all pure, then peaceable, gentle,
> compliant, full of mercy and good fruits,
> without inconstancy or insincerity.
> —James 3:17

I'M NOT SURE how much earth time has passed since my personal journey here began, but one thing is for sure: I have grown in my spirit and my awareness, beyond what I could have ever imagined.

As soon as Jill left, I walked around Rome, all the way to the Spanish Steps. Aside from the stunning view of the rooftops from above, I marveled at all the interesting people as they passed by. They would often stop to embrace one another and would glow on contact. It was breathtaking to observe. What an amazing thing God had created.

I walked to the bottom with ease and sat on a ledge surrounding the fountain created by Pietro Bernini, the father of the famous Gian Lorenzo Bernini, in 1629.

In the earthly realm, I would have just walked past all these people, perhaps with a small hello or a quiet nod. But now, it was like walking through an entire city filled with family members and close friends; I couldn't help but stop, greet everyone individually, and offer them a hug.

With every hug, I grew. I grew in awareness and knowledge—not to mention reeling more joy into my being, as if inhaling a deep breath of air into my lungs. On contact, I was now able to tell how long each spirit had been here by the amount of energy flowing from them. I could also sense that some spirts had more of a glow than others. *Perhaps I will have that brilliant glow in time.*

After finding a quiet place by the fountain, I sank into a deep meditative state, my mind searching for God's guidance on this journey. I saw flashes of faces I knew—people who died many years ago, people I'd love to see again.

Just not now.

It was hard to say if that gut feeling was my own or God's direction, but I couldn't commit to one single person who came to mind.

I began to wonder if there was an internal block of some kind preventing me from visualizing people I knew personally. The gravity of seeing them again felt superb and overwhelming. *Is it that I'm not strong enough yet?*

And that's when the thought came to me: *What if I try visualizing somebody I have respect for and would love to meet but don't have any personal ties to?*

"Okay," I said out loud to myself. "I've got a person in mind."

Shutting my eyes, I sat there and repeated this person's name over and over as I visualized everything I could about him. I'd never met him, obviously, but he made a huge impact on the world, and after studying him in school, I knew I had at least a semi-reliable mental image of his physical appearance to go on.

Eventually, I felt my surroundings change. The gurgle and splash of the fountain, the distant conversations, all faded away—replaced by the familiar hush of a breeze as it filters through a tall-standing oak.

And that's where I am now.

I'm back in Magnolia, at the picnic table. Eyes closed, breath held, and senses as acute as they've ever been. In my mind's eye, I can see the picnic table, the oak, the garden, the house . . .

And now, all I've got left to do is continue visualizing *him*. But what if two or more people visualize the same person at the same time? There are billions of souls in the afterlife. Can that person appear in two places (or more) at once? I leave this as a question for Micah and continue my visualization.

I see brown, slightly curly hair. A tanned complexion. Light eyes, high cheekbones, and a tall stature. I think of his name over and over in my mind, until at last, I decide it's time to open my eyes.

I realize, in addition to being back in Magnolia, that sitting across from me is Abraham Lincoln.

I guess, even after everything I've seen so far, I'd started to doubt visualization would work for me. But this man is real, and he certainly has that bright glow to him. I look at him, and he smiles and says, "Of course it works, Lou."

Shaking, I try to say something intelligent but only stammer out, "M-Mr. Lincoln?"

"You can call me Abe. Let's have a hug."

We stand and walk around the picnic table to embrace one another. His person is ungainly—over six feet tall, a little stooped in the shoulders, with long legs and arms. His head is over the average size, and his eyes are gray.

He places his top hat on the table, and we embrace. I try to anticipate what energy will flow into me as we embrace, but it goes beyond anything I could ever have imagined. The greatness of this man, now spirit, fills me and consumes me as we hug. I feel such a surge of honesty, humility, courage, justice, and grace.

"You are such a great man, Abe. I can't believe you are here in Magnolia with me." Pointing to my house as we sit, I tell him, "This was the house I grew up in."

"It's beautiful here: the big oak tree, the magnolia, the dogwoods, and all the rosebushes . . . . Ah! And there is Kingsley, sprawled out next to the rosebushes."

"You've met Kingsley, I take it."

"Indeed, yes, we've all met Kingsley." At the sound of his name, Kingsley pops his head up, looks over at us for a moment, then lays his head back down.

Looking back at Mr. Lincoln, I am compelled to tell him that in school, we made silhouettes of him.

After a deep laugh, he says, "Ha! You and a million others, apparently."

"When I was thinking about who I wanted to talk with next, you came to my mind, but frankly, I didn't think I could really do it. I am honored to be sitting here with you." I hesitate to call him Abe, but he did tell me to. "I am honored to be sitting here with you, Abe."

As Abe looks at me with his gray eyes, he reaches across the table and holds my wrist. "It is I who should be honored, Lou."

"You? Honored to talk to me? You're kidding, aren't you?"

"You are here, my friend. That means God wants you here, and soon you will see him and know that. And, in knowing that, you will know what you mean to him. And that, my good friend, makes me honored to be here with you on your journey."

"Well, I appreciate that, Abe. I was always so impressed by you as a person and a leader. I would quote you from time to time. My favorite was 'This too shall pass away. Never fear.' You always exemplified being a good man—a strong and brave and honest man."

"Thank you, Lou. In the earthly realm, I was fortunate to have some insight into God's plan, of which I was a part, as were you. Naturally, it was only insight at the time, but I sensed it to be much more. Having that insight made the difference for me. I saw past the temporary, earthly existence, but I also saw how it was connected to the eternal existence. Seeing that connection helped me strive to achieve justice and fairness at a time the world was in need of it. Being honest was a natural part of that—dealing with individuals and situations fairly, with truth. Heck, I never had a formal education, yet I became a lawyer and president—not easily, as you probably know."

I nod, rapt in the conversation we're having. And yet the handshaking nerves from earlier have faded, replaced by the comfort of familiarity. Indeed, it feels as though I'm just visiting with a longtime friend and not the world-renowned Abraham Lincoln.

He pauses, studying the oak tree, and says, "I was remembered for those things, but I was fortunate to be in the public. My vision, as I mentioned, was God's vision, and I saw that early on. Being here, Lou, you also must have led a good life. From our embrace, I was able to tell you're the sort of man who's fair. You're not one for preconceived notions or judgment, and I appreciate that about you. And if I felt that through our embrace, that means God knows it too."

My eyes tear up again. I wonder if I'll ever get used to feeling so understood. When I was alive, I never realized how rare it was to feel this way. The fact that Abraham Lincoln felt good traits in me, a nobody from South New Jersey . . .

Oh God, how do I come close to deserving this?

"We are spiritual beings, Lou. We have always been living expressions of God. Divine life has always lived in us. It's those divine qualities that make us who we are. In the earthly realm, people don't nurture their spiritual life as we do here—not only through prayer but also by finding the divine presence everywhere we go and in everyone we meet."

"I noticed, Abe, that many people I see here have a glow to them. Others, like me, are somewhat radiant, but it's not like the glow in many—and certainly in you."

Again, his gray eyes seem to pierce me as his pronounced smile widens. "My friend, you will also glow before you know it. And you will know why."

I have yet to leave the magnificent state of wonder I've been in since I left the hospital, and it just keeps compounding. Abraham Lincoln is telling me that so much more is ahead, and the joy I am feeling is overflowing . . .

What else can I ask him?

"Mr. Linc—I mean, Abe. There are many souls for me to meet, but since you have been in heaven for a while, I am sure you have grown significantly, and I was wondering if you would answer a question that has plagued me all my adult life."

"Yes, Lou, I know how you feel. You want to learn as much as possible. It's how we were created, so feel free. I don't know everything. I am also still growing. What is on your mind?"

"I know you weren't known as an astrophysicist and you are more of a people person, but I have always wondered about life on other planets. I mean, there are trillions of planets out there. From the souls you've met and your experience here in heaven, is there life on any of them?"

"That is indeed a new question for me," he says, chuckling. "And you are right, I have no background in astrophysics—is that what you called it? But I am sure such a person will tell you the same thing I will tell you—that is, if they are on this side of heaven. In fact, if you don't mind, I have someone I talk to from time to time in mind. I could bring him here now to address your question. He once said, 'The more I study science, the more I believe in God.'"

I don't how to react to Abe's suggestion other than to acquiesce to it, for I know who said those words. Abe closes his eyes and seems to be visualizing. When he opens them, he looks around, and just as he does, a man walks toward us. He has a dark mustache and brown-and-gray wavy hair and is holding a pipe. Yes, it's Albert Einstein. I do not know how to react other than just to be as I watch them embrace. When they separate, Abe introduces me to Albert and tells him I have a question.

I hesitate as Albert lights his pipe and looks directly at me. Every new experience here is unbelievable, yet it is real. I look at him and try to address him as intelligently as I can. "Well, ah, yes, so nice to meet you, Mr. Einstein."

"Just call me Albert, my friend. First, let's embrace." As we do, I feel a surge of energy flowing into my essence. When we separate, he looks at me and says, "So you were wondering about life on other planets. Is that it?"

I look at Albert, then at Abe, then back at Albert. I hesitate at first but then say, "Well, yes, I have always been curious about that."

"It's good to be curious, Lou. I always said we should learn from yesterday, live for today, and hope for tomorrow. The important thing is not to stop questioning, even here in heaven, but I will say that answers to our questions come a lot faster with an expanded consciousness. As far as your curiosity goes, whether there are aliens or not, we are all significant in God's eyes. You will see that more and more on your journey. Unfortunately, in the earthly realm, most speculation about intelligent extraterrestrial life leaves out God entirely. What I can tell you, Lou, without a speck of doubt, is that only God can create life. And as you progress through the dimensions of heaven, it will become crystal clear to you why he creates life. Consider these two truths. First, everything in the universe—heaven, earth, and beyond—owes its existence to God. Astronomers and other scientists have discovered many things about space—countless galaxies, incredible distances, and all kinds of phenomena we can barely understand. Yet nothing is as profound as those first words of the Bible: 'In the beginning God created the heavens and the earth.' God is that great."

"Yes, he is," I agree, smiling.

"The other truth is that although God created us in the earthly realm, we have rebelled against him and chosen to go our own way. We have rejected God, our creator, and we have paid a terrible price for our folly. This is why he sent his son to us. Through him and his example, he gave us hope that, despite our imperfections, we can still be with God in the spiritual realm forever. You are here, my friend. So you can be curious about life beyond heaven and earth, but we will celebrate all life God chooses to create. These truths and the ultimate truth I discovered as a young man have guided me throughout my life."

"The ultimate truth?"

Albert smiles sincerely and deeply. "Love. It dispels the darkness of conflict and loneliness with the light of harmony and togetherness. It is personal and sacred, human and divine, immediate and immortal. It is why God created life, and it brings him into the universe—in heaven and on earth."

"You are amazing, both of you, and you have enlightened me on my journey, for sure." Looking at Albert and still somewhat confused by his answer, I ask him, "So, Albert, if I understand you, there could be life on other planets, and if so, they were created by the same God who created us?"

"Yes—you understand me perfectly, Lou. I will leave you now. Enjoy your journey. Perhaps we will meet again."

As he walks away, I turn to Abe. "Thank you for bringing Albert here to address my question. I have another question before we part: Do people have homes here? I mean, where do you go?"

Abe expels a hearty laugh. "We go to our homes, Lou. You read the Bible from time to time, right? I felt it in our embrace."

"Well, yes, from time to time—certainly not cover to cover, but I have read parts and have also read and heard sermons that addressed sections of it."

"As spiritual beings, our true home is in the heart of God. In the Bible, however, God promises all those who believe a place in heaven—a home created just for them. Some versions of the Bible call it a room, others a mansion, but it's really a place God created specifically for us. What do you think mine is?"

I look at Abraham Lincoln sitting across from me, asking *me* a question, and can't help but grin stupidly. "A log cabin?" I guess.

Again, he laughs heartily. "Indeed, it is. I have a log cabin in the Appalachian Mountains of Kentucky, and that's where I go from time to time. I love my quiet time there. I still love chopping wood for the fire, and I get plenty of company—including Mary, who visits me from time to time. God knew exactly what I wanted in a home, and he knows exactly what you want. You'll see, Lou."

Abe stands, indicating our meeting is about to conclude, and I offer his tall frame a final embrace.

"Off to your cabin, I am guessing?" I ask.

"I am. I would say good luck on your journey, Lou, but I know this journey has nothing to do with luck. God bless you, son."

CHAPTER 11

In the Flow

> But while he was still a long way off, his father saw him and was filled with compassion for him; he ran to his son, threw his arms around him and kissed him.
>
> —Luke 15:20

AFTER MY TIME with Abraham Lincoln and a host of other spirits (some well known back in the earthly realm and some not so well known), it becomes clearer to me that here, we are all well known—to each other and certainly to God. Questions about this spiritual realm still come to mind, but thanks to having unlimited resources, they are resolved almost as soon as they surface.

I have come to realize that the spirits who seem to glow the brightest here have encountered God directly, and the light that shines from them comes from him. I also have realized God's light has always shone through us, but in the earthly realm, that light was something more felt than seen. The closer our awareness to his presence was, the brighter our internal light became. Every time we reached out to help in some way, our light not only shone brightly but grew stronger.

I've been told I will encounter God when the time is right. Of course, time has a new meaning here. Seconds, minutes, days, weeks—those all recede, replaced by a measurement that's impossible to describe. There is just a dynamic and awakening *now*. Imagine how easy it would be to appreciate the *now* if the past and future weren't there to taunt or entice or intimidate. That's how it feels here.

I know this *now* will lead me to my encounter with God, and I know it's coming, and I know that it will be overwhelming. Each spirit I encounter is astounding, and each embrace is like a wave of joy and peace that becomes a part of me that I pass on to others. My mind is not what it used to be, and my awareness is still expanding—my awareness of both the life I left and the life I am currently living.

Concern for those I left behind fades as I realize they too will live on and be with me, and I know that, in many ways, the grief they're experiencing in my loss is just one of the many important lessons taught by the earthly realm. When it's their time, they will embrace heaven, and they won't look back once they encounter such love. However, I have heard that exceptions can be made, occasionally, to provide our earth-dwelling loved ones signs to help them move on. Usually that's the duty of their guardian angel, but it isn't out of the question for a passed loved one to get involved.

Since embracing my new journey in heaven, I've had the chance to oversee Mike's new journey on earth. Thankfully, I was ninety-two, and he'd emotionally prepared for my passing, to an extent. I'd lived a good life, and that comforted him, but I just wish so badly that I could tell him personally how much there is to look forward to—that he'll see me again, along with his mother and brother. For now, it's important that he focus on his earthbound lessons. I take comfort in knowing that someday, I'll be one of the spirits dropping in to help him orient to heaven. Perhaps I'll be one of the first to meet him during his own experience of heaven, be it on a picnic bench in Magnolia or elsewhere.

In the meantime, I've come to adopt a sense of routine here. I don't ever have any sense of loneliness; I enjoy my solitude, just like President Lincoln said he still enjoys his time chopping firewood. Besides, I know I have the freedom and ability to meet anyone I want to—well, anyone who is in heaven. As I ponder that thought, a wave of gratefulness washes over me yet again. I am grateful that I am here and that my life pleased God in various ways—ways that were in alignment with love, light, and life, ways that many times went against what society and the culture were dishing out.

Today, I spent the morning doing what I normally do: enjoying coffee outside on the picnic table beside the large oak tree. Overlooking the expanse of one of my favorite places on earth, I inhale the scent of roses and sigh, a smile on my face.

I'll never get sick of it here.

After finishing my coffee, I decide to get up and walk around—I start off by going to the side of the house, looking at the place where I used to burn trash.

Who would have imagined I would be back here on this amazing journey? Thinking about what Abe told me—that throughout his life, he had more insight than others on God's plan—I have to wonder why some people back in the earthly realm have more insight than others when it comes to understanding God's plan. What might my life have been like had I known about all this—my guardian angel, the spiritual world, heaven, visualization, all of it? How could anyone *have* such insight? How did Abe acquire such insight?

If I'd had that insight, I sure would have been happier, and I certainly would have put a lot of effort into living a good life. I just thank God I lived a good enough life to get here. I think about losing Timmy and my wife and other grief I encountered in life, and I know for a fact that my relationship to loss would have been completely different had I'd known and trusted God's insight. I would have earnestly prayed that those who passed had made it to this eternal rest and that this perpetual light was shining upon them as it now does upon me and all those I meet here.

As I walk around the yard pondering all this and more, I see Kingsley lying down by the rosebushes, looking rather snug and relaxed.

"What are you doing over there, Kingsley?"

He lifts his head and looks at me as if to say, "Leave me be."

"What you got for me, Kingsley?" I crouch down and tempt him to come and get me. I have a lot more courage this time since he didn't rip me apart last time. In fact, he didn't even scratch me.

As Kingsley stands, facing me, I second-think that. *Damn, he's big.*

"Yeah, come on; I'm ready for you!"

Kingsley's walk turns into a jog as I brace myself. Before you know it, we are wrestling on the grass as I get my hugs in, but this time, I feel a transfer of tremendous energy—the kind I've been getting through my previous embraces with people but so much purer this time. This is much more intense and so good. After rolling around, I stand and walk back to the picnic bench. I look back at Kingsley; he seems content to just lie where he is.

I decide to take a walk on the railroad tracks by my home that run from Philadelphia to Atlantic City. As a child, I spent so many days just walking on these tracks. As I walk, I think of the spirits I've encountered here and decide it's time to meet another—my dad.

My dad died so young. He was only fifty-nine, and I was twenty-six, when he passed. I hardly knew him as a man. He never met my children, and all through my life, I missed him. I missed having a dad just be part of my and my family's lives. What I do remember about him is that he worked hard as a carpenter. He also served in the South Pacific in World War II. I always admired and respected him for that.

As I walk, I close my eyes and visualize him. I remember all the times he hugged me, and I feel the stubble from his rough face rub against my cheeks. I remember where he sat at dinner and the times I helped with house projects—painting, roof repair—and yes, he allowed me to climb a ladder onto the roof. I visualize his brown eyes and his light-brown skin from working outside. I open my eyes to watch my feet step from one railroad tie to the next, and eventually, I raise my head to observe the parked boxcars to the left and farther up the tracks.

And I see an image walking toward me.

As it gets closer, I see it is my dad. His hair is dark, and he is wearing bluish-green cotton pants and a white linen short-sleeve shirt.

With each step, I notice more and more about him. He is definitely glowing brighter than I am, and he is young—younger than any memory I had of him—and he is smiling. I have been looking forward to this embrace. We both open our arms and hug.

"Oh, Dad!" I feel his energy flowing into me as I feel his face stubble on my cheek. "I missed you so much!" We part from the deep, warm hug, and tears flow down my face as I look into my dad's eyes. "Oh, Dad, you died so young. You never saw Tim or Mike. Oh, and Mike's girls—they are so beautiful. I prayed you would take care of Timmy when he passed. Jill and I were never the same after that terrible day."

Then I hug him again, even tighter this time. When I finally release my hold, he smiles warmly and says, "I saw your children, Louie, and when you prayed for me to watch over Timmy, I felt those prayers, and so did God."

"You felt them?"

"Yes. Just like when we embrace here and feel each other's energy and essence flowing into us. Prayer is another form of expressing love, and God loves that, here in heaven and on earth. Your prayer for Timmy flowed into me and echoed throughout my being. All you wanted was to know he was safe and in peace."

"So prayer from the earthly realm can cause an effect here, like when we do the visualization thing?"

My dad nods. "Yes. As you are starting to see, our awareness continues to expand here. I felt your concern and love for Timmy. When you prayed to me to comfort him, naturally, you didn't know he was already being comforted by Camael, his guardian angel. And, as Micah told you, our guardian angels are messengers from God, so that comfort was coming from God. But I still felt your prayers, and I was with him and Camael as he made the transition, which he did beautifully. You've embraced him. You know how much he has grown and how much love he emanates."

"I just melted when I embraced him, Dad. I always felt he was at peace, but to hold him and feel that peace, it was . . . Well, it was just amazing, like everything else I've experienced here. Thank you for comforting him. I prayed from my heart. I just never knew how my prayers were being received. Now I know."

"And there is so much more, Louie, so much more."

"I'll take your word on that, Dad. Do you believe I sat down with Abraham Lincoln in our yard in Magnolia?"

Dad's smile turns into a smirk. "What did he think of our yard?"

I laugh. "He liked it, especially the rosebushes and dogwood trees. When I told him how honored I was to be in his presence, he told me he was honored to be in mine. So crazy."

"Not really, son. Abraham's spirit is still growing. All our spirits are growing. So, like all of us, he looks forward to embracing others and learning and growing from them."

I sigh, shaking my head. "I've never felt like a particularly religious man, nor have I felt like somebody who was particularly kind. Did I do what I thought was right as often as possible? Yes. But it does still sometimes blow me away that I'm here."

My dad's eyes soften, and he nods. "Many of us feel that way. But it wasn't that you'd memorized scripture as much as it was all the love you showed—the compassion, the empathy and kindness, the sympathy and forgiveness you gave to others. Many people exhibit these virtues in their lives, but each person is unique, and each exhibits them differently. Anyone can be kind, but how many ways did you convey that kindness? When someone embraces you here, they derive those unique virtue instances, and, in turn, grow spiritually. This was also true in the earthly realm, Lou, but unfortunately, more emphasis was placed on physical and mental growth than on spiritual growth. As the belief in God started to fade, so did the mechanisms he created for us—visualization, prayer, and helping each other grow spiritually through embracing."

"Yes, I see that. Wish I saw it back then."

"Well, Lou, apparently you saw enough of it to be here, and now you know why Abraham Lincoln was honored to meet you—as others will be too."

It's so refreshing, having this conversation with my dad in heaven. I am astonished to hear him articulate what he has learned here. He was a kid when he came to the United States from Italy. The idea of my spirit constantly growing as I embrace others is invigorating. The awareness of God filling me with peace and joy still brings tears to my eyes, making me want to fall on my knees and thank him.

Looking up at my dad and being rather curious, I ask him, "Who did you meet when you first passed, Dad?"

He stops walking and just looks at me. Finally, he says, "I thought about it for a while, but then it dawned on me who I had to meet—Yasu Hiyashi."

"Yasu Hiyashi? I never knew him. I guess that was before my time?"

"Yes, Lou, it goes back to World War II in the South Pacific, where I fought with the US Marines. I never talked much about it when I lived in the earthly realm. When I was in Saipan and on one of the other smaller Mariana Islands, I had some . . . very unpleasant encounters."

"It was World War II, Dad," I say sympathetically. "That was part of war."

"I was forced to kill Japanese soldiers," he goes on, his mouth a thin line. It was a new experience, seeing somebody in heaven still regret the choices they'd made in life—that, somehow, they still couldn't find it within themselves to move on. "And not from afar, like from an airplane or something—up close."

I knew my dad was in the war, but I was too young to know any particulars, especially about what he had to do to stay alive.

He continued. "After a skirmish in a foxhole was over, I looked at the Japanese soldier I killed at close range. His eyes were open but lifeless—not full of rage as they were less than an hour earlier. I took his Imperial Japanese Army infantryman's dog tag. It was brass, with a ring and string still attached. I kept it with me for many years, and I saw him throughout my lifetime—both his rage face and his lifeless face."

"Oh, Dad," I say, breathless. "I can't imagine what that was like."

"No, there is no way you could. But when I was doing my visualizations, I decided to visualize Yasu. Of course, I had no idea he was here." He huffs a laugh, as though still in shock that either of them—killers, even if required by war—is allowed to be in heaven. "But I visualized him anyway because I needed to speak to him, probably more than anybody else. And he appeared. We embraced and cried like babies as our essences flowed back and forth. I discovered he was more upset about me carrying that guilt all those years than I was about what I did."

"Amazing," I say, moved. "Amazing that God grants you both that closure."

Dad nods, offering a sad but grateful smile. "We have become close friends, and we met each other's families. He loved meeting Timmy, and he helped me with my transition. I want you to meet him down the road, after you . . . . Well, whenever you are ready."

"I cannot wait to meet him, Dad."

"There is so much love and joy here, Lou. Our spirits seem to absorb the love and joy around us. You are in the initial dimension of heaven, and heaven is the embodiment of that love and joy. The happiness of heaven exceeds that of the earthly realm, where all our joys were limited and fading—here, they are endless. There is a beauty and truth that will be revealed to you more and more as you proceed, not to mention the joy of meeting and knowing God."

I hug my father again, feeling the beauty and love and truth that has been revealed to me. I ask him, "Have you seen God, Dad?"

"Yes, Lou. Living here is living in the flow of love—the flow of God. That flow joins us with him. It's the greatest wonder we will ever know."

As we walk together on the tracks, my dad gestures toward the Magnolia house. "Let's go and see Micah, shall we?"

We cross over Atlantic Avenue and walk through the giant evergreens on the corner, emerging on the side of our house where the cement path leads to the yard. As we walk under the cherry and magnolia trees, we come out by the pink dogwood and see Micah sitting at the picnic table.

As we sit, my dad tells Micah, "You did a great job with my boy, Micah. Thank you."

"Well, it's you who deserve the thanks. You were a great father, Lou Senior." Micah turns to me. "How was your journey?"

Looking at my hands and arms, I notice I am a lot brighter than when I started my journey from the café in Rome. "I've learned so much, Micah. I see so much . . . . I feel so much," I pause a moment, looking for the right words. "I *am* so much."

Micah smiles as though I've said all the right things. "You certainly are, my friend. You certainly are." He then turns to my dad. "I think he is ready for the party. What do you think, Dad?"

"He is definitely ready, Micah."

Micah stands and says, "Well, let's go."

CHAPTER 12

Love Never Dies

> Love is the vital core of the soul.
> And of all you see, only love is infinite.
>
> —Rumi

AS THE THREE of us walk to the back door of my Magnolia home, I ask my dad, "Where is . . . ah, Samuel, your guardian angel?"

"After he helped me with my transition, he was reassigned, I guess you could say. I still talk with him from time to time, but he has another person on earth to guide."

I look at Micah, but before I can ask, he says, "Yes, Lou, I will be reassigned soon as well. You have come a long way and will soon be on your own. But, as you have seen and will continue to see, you are never alone, except when you want to be."

I can't begin to think of how much Micah has done for me since I came here and, for that matter, how much he did for me in my earthly lifetime. He taught me to visualize people and places and . . . well, he has been part of my eternal life from my conception. I look at him with appreciative yet sad eyes.

He returns the look and says, "It's been my pleasure, Louis. Let's go in."

We walk in the back door of my Magnolia house the way that I have countless times before in my life. The back door opens into the knotty-pine kitchen. The kitchen leads into a decent-size dining room with a large entrance to the living room—a room more like a banquet hall than a living room. A winding black staircase leads into the center of the big room—all carpeted in beige. I hear conversations coming from the dining room and the large living room.

I walk into the kitchen and see my mom approaching me. Just as our eyes meet, she smiles. She is much younger than the day she passed away in that hospital bed and so full of life—and yes, glowing brilliantly.

As we embrace, a wave of warmth and love floods my soul. I hold her and say, "Oh, Mom, how I've missed you!"

"I missed you too, baby. I knew you would be here, and here you are. At first, I worried so much about you. That's what moms do. But as I realized you would eventually be here, I just prayed that God and Micah would protect you and guide you toward that end. Many of your friends and family are here for you today, Louie. Timmy, Jill, your sisters, all your grandparents, and so many more."

Mom and Dad give each other a hug as we walk into the dining room. My three sisters, Linda, Angela, and Marie, attack me, hugging me. Linda says, "It's about time, Louie."

"I didn't think there was time here, Linda."

Angela chimes in. "There isn't, but we still looked forward to you being here with us."

"We knew you would be here, Louie," adds Marie. "This is a big day for you."

As Marie goes on talking, I notice a young man—maybe in his early twenties—standing where the dining room opens into the living room, smiling at me.

Just as I notice him, my mom calls the young man over, hugging him passionately. My mom then turns to me. "Meet Tommy, Louie. Your brother."

I look at him, then at my mom and dad, and before I can say a word, Tommy is hugging me. As he does, I become aware that Tommy is truly my brother—a brother who never made it to birth. I learn through our embrace that he's the brother who was deemed a miscarriage but a brother nonetheless. I sensed this also, to a degree, when I hugged my mom earlier. I sensed another soul had come to life through her in addition to my three sisters.

I hug Tommy, and my three sisters and parents join in, causing a whirlpool of energy transfer. When we finally break apart, Micah walks in and grabs my hand, leading me into the large living room.

"This is the last guidance I will provide you, my friend. Take your time and meet the rest of your family and friends. You know how to reach me if you need me. It's been such a pleasure being with you in the earthly realm and here in heaven."

My eyes tear up as I hug Micah. "How can I thank you, Micah? You know what's in my heart. I was so fortunate to have you throughout my life. I am sorry for any bad turns I may have made that went against your—

or, I guess I should say, God's—will, but I humbly thank you and God for an amazing life: both my earthly life and now my eternal life."

More tears flow when I release my embrace with Micah. As he walks away, I am flooded with more embraces from my grandparents, aunts and uncles, cousins, friends, and others I don't know or recognize who introduce themselves to me. One young Japanese man smiles at me as we embrace.

"Yasu?"

"That's me, Yasu Hiyashi. I am proud to meet you, Lou. I've heard so much about you."

As I hug Yasu, I look across the room and see my dad smiling at us. I also realize I am embracing a Japanese soldier from WWII. Did he speak English to me, or did he speak Japanese, and I heard it as English? Perhaps it's some sort of telepathic connection enabling communication. I decide it isn't important to know as long as there is communication.

"So nice meeting you, Yasu . . . so nice."

I wipe tears from my eyes as I part ways with Yasu and continue to greet and hug everybody present. Every embrace fills me with the essence of somebody else's soul, and it's better than anything I've ever felt.

By the time I've made my way around the room, it's glowing brilliantly, like a crystal or a cut diamond—light as bright as the sun itself, casting off holographic rays.

I regard one side of the room and spot a feast of fresh-baked bread loaves with dollops of whipped honey butter and a large plate of elegantly sliced ripe fruit. I spot an entire bushel of plums and even a full tray of the fudgy brownies I used to buy at the Magnolia Bakery.

Back when I was in the earthly realm, I often wondered if there was food in heaven. Now that I'm here, surrounded by so much love and light,

I realize that of course food is in heaven. It wouldn't be heaven without good food.

My Aunt Margarette walks up to me and says, "It is so nice seeing you here, Louie. You look deep in thought. Get a glass of wine or some food; it is amazing."

"Well, that's what I was just thinking about, Aunt Margarette. I used to ponder if there would be food in heaven."

"That's a good thing, right, Louie? Another one of God's blessings—food. But food here is no longer essential to sustain life. It's to enjoy fellowship and to celebrate together, forever, as we are doing today. It's another way of giving glory to God."

"Well, on that note, Aunt Margarette, I think I would like to enjoy a glass of that red wine with you." As my aunt and I sip some incredible red wine and chat, we are pleasantly interrupted several times to meet relatives and friends. It's so amazing embracing my distant relatives as well as cousins I grew up with and friends who go back to my Magnolia days—grade school and high school. As I look across the room, I start to laugh as I shake my head in a state of wonderment.

Aunt Margarette senses my fascination and after a sip of red wine, she asks me, "What is it, Louie?"

Looking back at Aunt Margarette, I gesture toward my Uncle Bill across the room having a conversation with Abraham Lincoln. "This is just too much."

"That's one way to put it, Louie, but believe me, there is much more ahead."

Just as she says that I hear trumpets sounding. I am not quite sure where they are coming from, but everyone starts moving to the sides of the room, leaving the middle of the floor empty. My dad comes over to me and takes my wine, places it on a table, and then takes my hand and leads me out into the center of the room. He walks back to the side of the room with the rest of my friends and family as I stand there. The room becomes very quiet, and I hear another set of trumpet blasts. Everyone kneels, so I also kneel. I feel like something wondrous is about to happen and think to myself, *What other wondrous thing could happen?*

Just as I think the room has reached the maximum brightness, the glow becomes even more brilliant. I just kneel there, looking at the entrance to the dining room and seeing what appears to be a . . .

Yes, it was Kingsley walking into the room, his tawny brown skin glowing, and his slightly darker yellow-brown mane undulating with each step. His face was aglow with his orange-brown eyes. So majestic, so powerful, so noble. I turn to look around; everyone is kneeling with their heads bowed. As I look back at Kingsley, he begins to transfigure into a—

I freeze. *What is happening? He is transfiguring into a . . . into a man.*

I start to look up slowly, my whole being trembling with anticipation. He is wearing light-brown cotton pants and a white linen three-quarter-sleeve shirt with no collar.

His presence emanates a warmth and compassion I've never experienced, even during my travels through heaven. His hair is a brownish red—kind of like a chestnut color, parted in the middle, then curling down to his shoulders. I hesitate to make eye contact, but I do. His face is without spot or wrinkle; his nose and mouth are perfectly formed; his beard is not too thick, the same color of his hair—not very long, but slightly forked.

I start to shake as we make eye contact.

His eyes are brown and clear and so piercing. He smiles at me as if he's known me my whole life—the way my dad smiled at me on the railroad tracks.

His presence takes hold of every part of me as I kneel before him and bow down, my head touching the floor. Tears flow from my eyes. How could I—yes, me, with so many flaws—be in front of the creator of life? I sense him walking closer to me. I knew this moment was coming, but the reality of it has sidetracked my whole being. Nothing could have prepared me for this! Eventually I manage to look up at him, and with all my strength, through my shaking and amid the flow of tears, I manage to speak. "My Lord and my God, have mercy on me—I am not worthy to be here."

He reaches down and touches my head, and as he does, I feel a tremendous flow of energy and warmth emanate from him. He reaches for my chin to lift my head up. As he does, I glance at his wrist. It is scarred, as if a spike had been driven through it. I realized at that moment a level of love that runs deeper than anything I have ever felt. Why would God make such a sacrifice for me, a virtual nobody, and give me eternal life? I never got the sacrifice thing, only glimpses from time to time, but now I understand that this sacrifice is the only way to comprehend the depth of such love. As he lifts my face, I look up at him. When we make eye contact, more tears flow. He continues to smile at me. "Rise, my son."

I stand up slowly, and he opens his arms. I embrace him. There are no words to describe the flow of pure light and love from him. When I first embraced Timmy after so many years, I thought I was going to burst from the love. Hugging Jill in Italy, my mom in the kitchen, and my dad on the railroad tracks all revealed a deep current of love, but nothing surpasses the love of Jesus holding me. I just want to stay here and absorb it all. He moves his hands to my shoulders as we loosen our embrace and says, "Welcome, Louis. Let's take a walk. You have been through a lot, my son. I was so happy when you met Timmy and Jill again."

"There are no words that I can think of to describe that feeling. Thank you." I hesitate to address him, but I see him smile, sensing my hesitation, so I say it. "Thank you, Jesus! I am sorry for all my doubt and for abandoning you during those times. I just couldn't understand."

"You were not meant to understand during that time, my son, but you never abandoned me. I heard your prayers, and I knew your heart."

Yes, I am walking with Jesus out the back door of my Magnolia home—the same door I blew through as a kid a thousand times before jumping on to my trusty black Schwinn. We walk down the steps and bear right, walking under the beautiful magnolia tree. I smell the aroma of its blossoms. Their fragrance seems stronger than I remember.

We turn toward the giant evergreens, where my dad and I walked not so long ago when we left the railroad tracks and walked across the street toward our house.

"Despite the tragedies in your life, Lou, you've lived a good life. You were kind to people. You were concerned for them, especially the meek and vulnerable. You were empathetic and you reached out when you could. You were a good man, a good husband, a good father, and a good worker. No, you were not perfect in any of those roles, but you were good and kind, and you respected others, and you respected life—all life. Well, except for that turtle."

I look up at Jesus through my tears, not knowing what to say, but I see he is smiling. "I am sorry about that," I say earnestly. "That was childish and mean."

"You enjoyed your childhood in Magnolia, didn't you?"

"Oh yes, it was the best."

"I wanted you to start your heavenly journey here because you loved it so much. You were a free spirit here, taking in all of life—your family, friends, nature, all of it. Without knowing it, my son, you were as close to heaven as anyone could be."

"Yes, it was magnificent. Thank you for allowing me to grow up here and for all you provided me. I know I wasn't that religious. Sorry about that."

"There is no religion here, Louis, only love. It's what life is and what it was meant to be—both here and on earth. I infused people with this love and wanted them to experience it and understand that it is love that makes them different from all my other creations. I knew it would take time for people to understand how much I loved them, but I never wanted to create a world of robots. I created very real people, and I wanted them to experience love in a very real world—not a perfect world, but a real world with all its faults. Love needs freedom; that's why you were so close to it in Magnolia. I intended all people to be free. I wanted them to understand love in the real world, and through that love, I wanted them to know me. In knowing me, they would understand I would never limit their lives to the earthly realm. I created heaven and earth and wanted them to understand that heaven and earth are connected. Whatever leads people to that understanding is good. Whether it is through religion or not, I made that desire part of each person. You've seen glimpses of it in your life, my son, and when you did, you were very close to me, and I was extremely happy for those times."

I cannot even begin to understand the depth of what Jesus has shared with me as we walk, but I do understand the depth of the love he speaks of. I know that understanding grows with each soul I encounter and embrace here in heaven. Yes, I only had glimpses of such love back in the earthly realm, but thank God for those glimpses—they were enough to get me here. I think of some of the books that had a major impact on my life and contributed to what Jesus is telling me now as I walk through evergreen trees in Magnolia or in some part of heaven.

When we reach the end of the evergreen trees, there is no Atlantic Avenue, nor are there any railroad tracks. I only see green rolling hills with grapevines and, at the top, a winery and a small cabin made of wood and stone.

As we walk through the vineyard, I look at Jesus and all I can think to say is "Why a lion?"

Jesus laughs loudly, which startles me but also eases my overall state of mind, causing me to laugh as well. "I thought you would get a kick out of that," he said. "I did enjoy pouncing on you when you were climbing your Tarzan rope for dear life."

Our laughter subsides, and I say, "Well, yes, I was scared. You definitely got me. How did everyone back in my living room recognize you when you walked in as a lion?"

"I've appeared to my people in many forms, Lou. Everyone present today has an expanded awareness. They would recognize me no matter what form I chose to take."

"Will I get that way too?" I ask, hopefully.

"Yes, of course." Jesus pauses for a moment, then adds, "Everyone is always aware of my presence, even in the earthly realm—it just takes practice to recognize me anywhere and everywhere."

"I'm sure you appeared to me on earth, and I missed you more than a few times."

"Well, we are together now, my son. Let me show you the winery."

"The winery?"

"I know you've always had a passion for wine and wineries and how you longed to have one or at least work at one, so I thought this might be a good place for you to start."

"To start?"

"Yes, what did you think those prayers 'rest in peace' meant?"

"I guess I never thought about it."

"Well, they don't mean rest in the sense of cessation from work. Rather, they mean rest in the sense of peace of soul, joy, and profound happiness. This is the uninterrupted rest you have now, Louis. I meant for my people on earth to have this rest—to release their concerns in prayer and to relax and be calm. To be enfolded in my loving presence. It was my intention, but it became hidden in the midst of various societal and cultural pressures. But you don't have those pressures now, and you are aware of my presence, Louis, and that awareness will grow and bring you everlasting peace. That's the peace you experience here with each embrace."

Everlasting peace? Hearing this from Jesus takes away much of my concern for those I left behind. The only part left is that they live their lives in a way that will bring them to this same everlasting peace.

Jesus looks at me and says, "They will."

As we walk closer to the winery, a man walks out to meet us. When he gets closer, he kneels and bows to Jesus.

"Oscar! Please rise, my son, and meet Louis."

Oscar, a gentle and lively Latino man who appears to be in his thirties, gets to his feet, and we embrace. Immediately, Oscar's sense of peace and joy floods my soul. He is wearing what appears to be loose jeans and a tee with beige work boots. He has dark features with dark-brown hair with a matching mustache. At the end of our embrace, he greets me with "Welcome to In Vino Veritas Vineyard, Louis. We call it the Three Vs."

"This is such a beautiful winery and vineyard, Oscar."

Jesus puts his arm around me and says, "Oscar's first assignment was to run this winery. Now his assignment is to teach you how to run it, Louis."

I've always daydreamed about running my own winery. I look around and remember Laura telling me about her assignment in heaven and think this assignment is perfect for me.

"Thank you so much. I hope I will do you both justice and do a good job here."

"Oscar will have you up to speed in no time, and I mean that literally." We all laugh. Jesus bids Oscar goodbye for now, and then takes my hand, walking me toward the cabin at the top of the hill. As we approach the cabin, a dog runs out from the back of it and down the hill toward us. It appears to be a golden retriever.

As it gets closer, I recognize her. "It's Emma!" We greet and roll all over the green grass, Emma licking my face. Eventually, she calms down, and I get up, my face wet as I look at Jesus.

"I know how much you loved that dog, Louis. Now, let's take a look at your cabin," he says.

"This will be my cabin?"

"Yes, for now, as you settle into this first dimension of heaven, overlooking the vineyard and the winery. I think it's a good start for you."

Apparently, tears still flow in heaven, or at least in this first dimension of heaven, because all this is just too overwhelming for me. I kneel again in front of Jesus, and as I do, Emma thinks I want to play, so she is all over me. But I tell her to sit, and she does—as she always did back in the day. Looking up at Jesus, through my tears, I tell him, "This is too much. I don't deserve all this."

Calmly, he looks at me and offers me his hand. I stand, and he tells me, "Sure you do—and more. Now, go check out your cabin, and then let's get back to the party. I want you to taste the wine from your winery.

It's being showcased back in Magnolia, unless, of course, your family and friends drink it all."

I walk to my cabin, again without words—fireplace, bookshelves, so much of everything I had imagined. I say to Jesus, "It's . . . well, it's perfect."

"It's a good start. Your place to come anytime you need to be here. You know how to meet people. You know how to travel. You know how to pray—not just to me, but to anyone here or on earth."

"Anyone on earth?"

"Yes, their guardian angels will hear you and try their best to get your message across."

I think of Mike, whom I've had to leave behind, along with so many others. I know it's only part of their journey now, grieving my death—the same way it was part of my journey to grieve Timmy's and Jill's and my parents' and so many others. More than anything, I want to give Mike some sign there really is a heaven.

Jesus asks me, "If you could get a message not only to Mike but to everyone, what would it be?"

I can't believe Jesus is actually asking me this question. "Well, I don't know what messages I could send that you haven't already delivered in one form or another, but from my point of view, I would simply tell everyone that it's all real. You are real. Heaven is real. Love is real. And I would tell them that life everlasting is real, and they should plan on being here."

Jesus smiles. "And how can they do that?"

"By embracing everyone they encounter, treating them as vulnerable and in need of love and kindness. And then I would tell them to exercise that love and kindness. I would also tell them to smile more, to show their faith and their hope, for eternal peace and happiness is just ahead."

Jesus continues to smile. "I like that, Louis. What do you say we get back to the party?"

"I say yes!"

* * *

A few months have passed back in the earthly realm. Mike has tried to keep his promise to his dad by stopping by a small chapel every Wednesday during his lunch hour. He usually sits in one of the last pews in the back and just talks to God out loud since most days, he is alone. On this day, he is feeling lonely and frustrated as he prays.

"Here I am, Lord. You can't say I haven't tried to honor my father by trying to, in his words, 'keep the door open.' I have read parts of the Bible, and I know not to ask for a sign, but perhaps just a little one? All I ask is to know my dad is safe and at peace. I hope he is with Timmy and my mom and with you."

Mike looks at his watch and starts to get up when a man walks in and sits across from him to pray. Mike decides to sit back down and watch the man. After a while, he decides it's time to get back to work, but before he can stand, the man gets up and begins to walk out. Before he leaves the chapel, he turns to Mike and says, "Your dad is in peace, and yes, so are Timmy and your mom, Mike." With that, the man leaves the chapel.

Mike jumps up and walks quickly out the same door to talk to this man, but he is nowhere in sight. Only Mike's car is parked by the chapel. Mike looks around the chapel and walks completely around it, but no one is present. Looking up to the sky, he says, "Thank you, Pop! Thank you!" Tears start to roll down his face as he goes back into the chapel to thank his dad and God in a proper fashion. When he walks in, he sees a small yellow object on the seat where the man was praying.

As Mike gets closer, his eyes can't believe what he sees. Sitting on the pew is a Mallo Cup.

AFTERWORD

I TRULY HOPE you enjoyed my brief view of heaven. It's all about hope, love, peace, joy, and yes, life. And why not? God loves us beyond any words we can come up with. We get glimpses of the extent of his love here in the earthly realm, but our citizenship is in heaven.

Jesus said,

> In my Father's house there are many dwelling places. If there were not, would I have told you that I am going to prepare a place for you? And if I go and prepare a place for you, I will come back again and take you to myself, so that where I am you also may be.
>
> —John 14:2–3

One of the criminals hanging on the cross next to Jesus said, "Jesus, remember me when you come into your kingdom." Jesus replied, "Amen, I say to you, today you will be with me in Paradise" (Luke 23:43).

THOMAS FARGNOLI

For I know well the plans I have in mind for you—plans for your welfare and not for woe, so as to give you a future of hope.

—Jeramiah 29:11

Please check out my website: www.thomasfargnoli.com.

Please feel free to email me at tom-magic@comcast.net.

We are loved beyond our capacity to understand—God bless you.

If you enjoyed *Magnolia—A View of Heaven*, you'll enjoy Thomas Fargnoli's two other books, *Wisdom from the Wick* and *The Deacon—An Unexpected Life*, Fargnoli's memoir.

WISDOM FROM THE WICK

No one seems to remember when John first started coming to the Wick. Who is he? Why the Warwick Tavern? His discussions on life and faith don't seem appropriate for a neighborhood tavern.

Despite that—or perhaps because of it—people come to him and welcome his views, which always seem uncannily tailored to what they need to hear. The crazy thing? They didn't come to the Wick to have any such conversations; they came to have a few drinks and laugh with friends. At least, that's what Bob, a Wick's regular, thought when he stopped in one night.

But there was something about John that drew people to him. When Bob sat down next to John that night, he didn't yet realize the unexpected path John would set him on. Over a couple of months, John, Bob, and a handful of other regulars discuss and witness the power of prayer, God's graces, hope, faith, and so much more.

So pull up a stool at the bar, order a drink from Al, and remember—open your mind, your spirit, your heart, and your soul. John will lead you through a journey of faith, hope, joy, and light.

THE DEACON—AN UNEXPECTED LIFE

We often end up living an "unexpected" life. Yet through it, glimmers of hope, faith, love, and peace find their way.

After being married for forty years and serving the Catholic Church as a deacon for the last five years, leaving the diaconate was the last thing on my mind.

Never did I expect to be a suicide survivor. Grieving the loss of my wife was difficult enough, but with suicide, the grieving was much more intense. Being a deacon in the Catholic Church intensified that grieving even more.

Being alone was never a problem for me, but true loneliness was something new. It came with a realization that I didn't have anyone to share my life with anymore, and, most dauntingly, because of being a deacon, it came with a sense of permanence—knowing this was my life now.

The Catholic Church made it clear. I could not stay a deacon and pursue another loving relationship that could lead to marriage. I was aware of the rule, but after two years of discernment, I couldn't seem to make a decision. This battle put me into the hospital for open-heart surgery. Finally, with God's help, I made my decision.

Rick, a local reporter, wanted to interview me with regard to my diaconate experience and how I came to that decision. He turned out to be more than a reporter. This is my true story. Through it, I hope glimmers of hope, faith, love, and peace find their way through your clouds as well.

Proceeds go to Suicide Awareness.

www.ingramcontent.com/pod-product-compliance
Lightning Source LLC
Chambersburg PA
CBHW011522070526
44585CB00022B/2502